Fractured Parables

Fractured Parables

*And Other Tales
to Lighten the Heart
and Quicken the Spirit*

A. Kenneth Wilson

Crest Books
The Salvation Army National Publications
Alexandria, Virginia

© 2001 The Salvation Army

Published by Crest Books, Salvation Army National Publications
615 Slaters Lane, Alexandria, Virginia 22314
(703) 684-5500 Fax: (703) 684-5539
www.salvationarmyusa.org

Printed in the United States of America

Cover and book design by Kristin B. Griffin

Library of Congress Catalog Card Number: 2001 089163

ISBN: 0-9704870-1-0

To my wife Charlotte and daughter Kristina—
my most ardent supporters and toughest critics, without whose
encouragement none of this would have happened.
And the adventure continues ...

Contents

———— ◆ ————

Contents

Preface

Rather than wait until I am a retired officer or dead and gone, I thought I would put some my literary nonsense in one place so I could keep track of it. It may not be as extensive as the collected works of Shakespeare or Commissioner Samuel Logan Brengle, but it is fun.

It all began in the pages of *The Musician*. Because I have been a Salvation Army musician since I was 10 years old and have an abiding love for Army brass band music, *The Musician* was the logical place to start contributing articles for publication. They were looking for material and offered a forum for my slightly off–center humor.

Brigadier Ron Rowland, former editor in chief and fellow musician, said to me, "Ken, if you send me a couple more articles, I think I can use them." What he did was open the flood gates to a whole new way of life and new opportunities for ministry. Sadly, *The Musician* has ceased to be, but it was fun while it lasted.

Since then portions of this material have appeared in *The War Cry* in the United States, the United Kingdom, Australia, South Africa and Canada; *El Grito de Guerra* in Mexico and South America; as well as *The Salvationist*, *Good News*, *The Officer*, audio scripts and other devotional materials in several other places.

Thank you for reading this book and sharing your reactions with me— you have made my parents very happy to see a return on their investment in my education. *The boy can finally manage to put a sentence together ... and type his own papers!*

Fractured Parables

I.

———— ◆ ————

Fractured Parables

At times it is both fun and beneficial to change the time and space or circumstances of events of the Bible. The people of that age were as real as we are today. We tend to consider them as little more than quaint people with quaint stories from a time that has little or nothing to do with where we are today. We do well to view them in a new light.

I must give thanks to the very hip and innovative *Rocky and Bullwinkle Show* that featured a segment entitled "Fractured Fairy Tales" narrated by Edward Everett Horton. Those creative cartoon re–tellings of classic children's stories were the inspiration for these re–tellings of Scripture classics.

Proverbs tells us that "a cheerful heart is good medicine, but a crushed spirit dries up the bones" (Prov. 17:22). So open up ... and say, "Ahhh!"

Raiders from the Sky

"A farmer went out to sow his seed. As he was scattering the seed, some fell along the path; it was trampled on, and the birds of the air ate it up. Some fell on rock, and when it came up, the plants withered because they had no moisture. Other seed fell among thorns, which grew up with it and choked the plants. Still other seed fell on good soil. It came up and yielded a crop, a hundred times more than when it was sown" (Luke 8:5-8).

"Listen up you bunch of gold–bricking goof–offs!" barked the master sergeant. Tough as nails, Sarge had drilled hundreds of green recruits, turning them into "lean, mean" fighting men. His tunic, liberally sprinkled with medals and campaign ribbons, bore tribute to his courage under fire.

"I hope your stay with us has been memorable, gentlemen. I want you to know that I believe you are now trained to my satisfaction."

I was never quite sure if Sarge drilled us hard out of concern for our survival in combat or whether he merely got a kick out of being mean.

Again came the familiar parade ground shout.

"I trust you learned and will remember well," he bellowed. "You came here as maggots. You go away men. We have pushed, prodded and hammered you until you are no longer the flabby, weak–willed civilians we started with. Now you are the finest fighting men I have ever had the honor to lead."

Wow, I muttered to myself, *a compliment from the Sarge.* They were very few and should be savored. But I didn't speak out loud for fear that even now he might make us clean the barracks with a toothbrush as he had done when we were raw recruits.

Sarge jolted me back from my daydreaming by announcing that orders for our first combat assignment had just come through. As bad as boot camp had been, it was still a game. Now Company C of the 83rd Airborne Rangers was going to war.

None of us got hurt too badly during basic training. Oh yes, Dinglemeyer nearly got flattened by a runaway backhoe and Agronsky got dehydrated during a bivouac in the hot summer sun. I knew that some of these guys I had trained with and liked so much wouldn't be coming back.

Mid–April found the men of Company C in a standard transport aircraft, cramped and hot as usual. We never flew in the spacious new aircraft. No, we always got the relics that smelled of leather, canvas and mildew. As paratroopers, we knew we would soon be in the drop zone. The fresh air would be a welcome change from the stifling heat of the aircraft.

I tried to take my mind off the jump. Sure, guys got killed in combat but it always happened to the other guy. It couldn't—or at least I hoped that it wouldn't—happen to me.

Old Sarge was right there with us.

"Check your equipment," came the order. "Drop time—five minutes to target!"

I checked and re–checked my gear and parachute for what seemed the hundredth time. All was in perfect order.

I inventoried all my other assorted supplies too—entrenching tools, rifle, canteen, rations, first aid kit, signal flares, radio—all set and secure.

I prayed that the person who packed my parachute did it carefully and not on his way out the door on payday.

Oh well, if it didn't open I'd be the first to know. It would only hurt for a little while—after the big thud at the bottom of a free fall of several thousand feet. My attempt at humor didn't cheer me up as much as I had hoped it would.

"Two minutes to drop—red light ON!"

Just two minutes—120 ticks of my digital watch. Strangely enough, above the noise of the aircraft I could still hear the pounding of my heart.

"One minute to drop—Hook up—Stand in the door! Prepare to jump!"

This was it: the point of no return. Once the green light came on, I had to go through with it, like it or not. If I hesitated at all, I knew that I'd get the point of Sarge's boot right in the backside.

"GREEN LIGHT—GO, GO, GO!"

At Sarge's command, C Company fell into the dark emptiness, one after another as wave after wave of uniformed commandos filled the early morning sky.

As I fell faster and faster waiting for the chute to open, I thought about those roller coaster rides I loved as a kid. Pretty tame compared to this.

It was only a few seconds of free fall, but it felt a lot longer as the green earth seemed to rush up to squash me like a bug.

As the chute snaked out of the backpack and made a graceful silk streamer above my head, I prayed that it would soon pop open and slow my runaway descent.

"C'mon chute. Let's get with it!"

Although I had jumped before, I was thrilled to feel the shoulder–jarring jolt as the big chute finally popped open. It hit with such force that I thought it would yank me right out of my boots. As I gently drifted to earth, I saw my buddies all around me dangling from the shroud lines like spiders in a web.

Our objective was a small, open field removed from the main battle area. A rear guard action, they called it. I kept wondering what significance this tiny piece of real estate held in the scope of the war. But it didn't matter. Our orders were to land, dig in and defend our position at all costs.

I was one of the lucky ones. I landed on a small patch of soft, brown earth. Others of my company landed in trees, rocks, weeds and swamp.

I quickly scrambled to my feet, just as Sarge had taught us, while pulling down the swirling canopy of the parachute. I popped the release buckle and swung up and engaged my weapon in defense just as I had done in hundreds of training sessions before.

"Seedman! Private Seedman!"

It was Sarge. He was tough, but was I glad to see him!

"Drop the pack, boy. We have orders to dig in right here. Get busy. I'll go check on the others."

I really worked up a sweat digging that hole. But I knew I had better get a good defensive position in case we were attacked by the enemy.

Before long, Sarge was back.

"Seedman," he growled, a look of concern in his eyes, "Cornwallis, Bean and Wheatly—I can't find them."

That was strange, for they had jumped just before me. I had seen Wheatly drift off to the left toward some heavy weed and thicket. Bean got caught in a strong cross current and ended up almost by the shoulder of the road, several hundred yards away from my position. As for Cornwallis, I feared the worst, because I never saw his chute open. I prayed for them all. We remained buddies through many a close call.

The day passed uneventfully as we reinforced our position until darkness came. By 2100 hours—9:00 pm for civilians—it was so dark and quiet that one could almost taste the fear, as if every shadow concealed an enemy soldier. With genuine white–knuckled panic, I gripped the stock of my weapon to prevent my future from coming to an abrupt halt. I heard the croak of a few frogs off in the distance along with the sing–song chirp of a cricket or two. I listened and prayed for dawn.

Sheltered from the elements, my hole afforded me an excellent position where I could see the enemy long before they could see me.

As I sat there I reflected on the fact that when times are good and life is easy we often forget about God. A few minutes of prayer seem like an agonizing eternity. But during that first desperate night alone and in danger, prayer gave me an inward sense of comfort and peace within that superceded the dangers of war.

"Lord, please help me not to run. Help me to be thankful for each day. And whether I make it or not, I'll still praise You."

After the longest night I had ever experienced, the first warm rays of sunlight glistened over the mountain behind my foxhole. I savored having survived the jump and my first night in combat.

As I sat in my foxhole cleaning my weapon, Sarge came by to check on my progress.

"Seedman, you did a good job of getting set up here. We may be using this area as our command post. You did real well, son."

"Sorry I was hard on you before," he continued. "Back at basic if I had been your buddy and kept you out of every dangerous situation, you'd probably be dead by now."

I wondered why he was telling me all this. "What happened to the other guys?" I asked.

"Seedman, you are the only man from your squad to make it alive. Wheatly landed in heavy weeds and swamp. He was hopelessly tangled and couldn't even get clear enough to fire his weapon. The enemy just cut him down. Bean hit the hard pack just by the road and broke his leg. He wasn't able to find cover. He tried to fight it out, but there were too many of them."

I had liked old Bean. He was plain and ordinary with no special talents or exceptional abilities, but he had a laugh that could lift even the most depressed spirit.

He was my best friend, and I missed him already.

Although I didn't want to hear about Cornwallis, I knew I'd never be at peace until I found out.

"Cornwallis never made it—never saw his chute open. A few of the men found his body where he landed on the rocks. It wasn't pretty. He was so far out that the buzzards got to him before we could."

Four brave friends went off to war, yet only one survived to tell the story. The war didn't last much longer, and we had played a big part. Just a few months after our initial invasion, it was all over. Thousands of us landed in that field, and the enemy could not drive us out.

We jumped as raiders from the sky, but we stayed to bring peace to a war–scarred land. My buddies would have been proud.

Does Anybody Here Speak Donkey?

Jesus asked, "'Which of these three do you think was a neighbor to the man who fell into the hands of robbers?' The expert in the law replied, 'The one who had mercy on him.' And Jesus told him, 'Go and do likewise'" (Luke 10:36–37).

I like working for the boss. He's the best employer I've ever had. And boy have I had some doozies! After all, being a donkey is not an easy business.

Some days we haul cargo. Some days we haul people. Most days we get beaten, as a matter of course. No wonder we have developed a stubborn streak. Any self–respecting donkey needs to fight back once in a while.

The boss is great, though. He treats me with kindness and generosity. Whenever he stops to eat, he feeds me too. I sleep in a snug barn that keeps the weather out—a nice change from some of the other mean masters who left me out in the sun or in the rain for days at a time.

We have just left Jericho after three days there on business—something about import–export. The boss is taking back some valuable samples of merchandise for the new fall line back home.

I sure wish we didn't have to travel down this awful stretch of road outside of town again. Almost every day the news carries stories of travellers being robbed, beaten and murdered along this piece of road. It is a favorite haunt for all the thieves, goons, creeps and weirdos in the district. I wish there was another route we could take to get home safely.

It scares me, but it is the shortest route. Oh well, we had a good night's rest, and we should be well out of Dead Man's Gulch long before dark. I sure don't want to tangle with those robber gangs at night. Boy, this is just like in those old cowboy movies. Someone out in the desert says something like, "It's quiet." "Yeah," his partner agrees, "too quiet—and bad things happen."

I have no sooner thought this to myself, because no one here speaks donkey, when thieves swoop down and hit the boss in the head with a rock.

"Haw, haw ... haw, hee, hee ..." I bellow as loud as I can to scare the assailants. But they keep right on coming.

Six of the meanest, ugliest, nastiest humans I have ever seen are beating up on the boss. They are punching and kicking the poor guy mercilessly. One of the biggest goons tosses him through the air like a rag doll. Then one of them eagerly asks if he can kill the boss. "He has seen us and can identify us. I don't like leaving behind witnesses. I don't plan on spending any time in a jail cell or dancing at the end of a rope."

Another says, "Aw, leave him alone. He probably can't identify us. He's out cold. And by the time he comes to, we'll have all his stuff and be long gone."

Finally the leader of the gang chimes in. "He's banged up pretty good. In a few hours we'll be long gone. Why should we risk a murder rap? Let's leave him to the desert sun. By the time the buzzards get through with him, there won't be any evidence at all."

Chuckling to themselves, feeling very satisfied with their loot of stolen merchandise and satisfied that the boss can not cause them further inconvenience, they go on their way. They flee, exulting in their escape.

Oh my goodness. The boss is a mess. He is covered with blood and bruises. I don't know much about medicine, but I know he is in bad shape.

C'mon boss, I think, We have to get you out of here and get to a doctor. Get up, I'll help you.

Rats! This is terrible. He's unconscious and I can't pick him up and put him on my back. Maybe someone will come along and give me a hand. Then maybe I can get him to a doctor. If we don't find some help fast though, we may not make it. He may die and leave me out here in the middle of nowhere to be caught by those thugs again.

Hey, this is fortunate. Here comes a Temple priest. He works for God and is a very religious man. Surely he'll stop and give me a hand in getting the boss some medical attention.

"Haw, hee, haw ..."

I keep forgetting—he doesn't speak donkey. He must think I am out of my head, braying and jumping around like this.

Oh good—he sees me. Hey fella—over here!!

I can't believe it. He looked right here at the boss and me and kept right on going. He saw the boss's wounds and all the blood, so he can't assume he's just taking a nap. I can't believe his attitude. It's as if we were invisible.

If this is an example of how humans treat each other, I'm glad to be a donkey. And to think ... they call *me* a jackass.

So now what am I supposed to do? It sure is hot.

But look ... this is great ... another human is coming. This is terrific. Our problems are over. This one is a Levite. Surely he'll stop to lend a hand.

Hey buddy—over here. C'mon over and give us a hand won't you please? When am I going to learn ... these people aren't smart enough to learn donkey. All I can do is jump and bray and hope he comes over to investigate the commotion.

He's crossing over to the other side of the road. I can't believe it—not again! He acts as if people lie by the side of the road covered with blood all the time.

You rotten bum. It's not like the boss is from another planet or something. He's a good, God–fearing, tax–paying, responsible, family man. You have to help him or he won't ever get to see his family again.

I tell you, I have no respect for these selfish humans at all. How good can their God be if His people treat each other like this?

We've been out here for hours now, and I feel as if my brain is starting to cook. My tongue's thick and swollen from thirst, and my mouth tastes like a camel just walked through it, and you know how dusty those camels can be.

The boss has been out cold for hours now. A couple more hours of this and we'll both be food for the buzzards.

I never thought it would end this way. I've had my share of bad times, but I never thought the boss would be left out here to die with two supposedly good men ignoring him.

There hasn't been anyone along in hours—not since the Levite. Hold on a minute. I do see someone coming down the road. I can't quite make out the style of dress. If it's those robbers again we're both doomed.

Oh no ... our luck can't be that bad. It's worse than I thought. It's a Samaritan. The boss told me that some Jews hate the Samaritans so much that they won't even walk on the same side of the road, or won't even speak to them. He'll take one look at the boss and me and keep right on going. And he has a Samaritan donkey too!

Oh well ... nothing ventured, nothing gained.

"Haw, haw ... hee, haw ..."

This guy seems to sense that something is wrong, and he's coming over to find out what it is. This is incredible. He's getting out his first aid kit and working on the boss's wounds! This is wonderful. I thought Samaritans were supposed to be enemies and here this man is treating us like friends and family.

"Here we go, donkey. I've done as much for your good master as I can out here. We need to get him some proper medical attention. Donkey ... do you think you are strong enough to walk?" he asked.

Walk?—you delightful man—put the boss up on my back and I'll hoof it out of here like the winner of the Kentucky Derby!

"You won't have to carry him. You can rest a bit. My donkey can carry your master."

It was the most wonderful ending to the most horrifying experience of my life. This Samaritan man picked us up on the road after two others passed us by. The Samaritan fellow took us to an inn and cared for the boss. He gave me some oats and fresh straw and plenty of water ... cool, clear water. He left money so we could be taken care of after he left. And before anyone could thank him for his kindness, he was up and gone, just like the Lone Ranger.

There was something unique about that man. He's someone I'd like to have for a friend—even if he can't speak donkey.

The Ultimate Yuppie

"Fear God and keep His commandments, for this is the whole duty of man" (Eccles.12:13).

MEMORANDUM
FROM: The Royal Palace
TO: Anyone Who Cares to Read and Heed

Well, I finally made it. I am a Yuppie—a young upwardly mobile urban professional. Actually, I am just a product of my society that places a high importance on success and acquisition. I have all the money, power and toys I can use. Along the way, I found that the more I got, the more I wanted. The problem is, now that I have it all, I don't know what to do with it.

Let me tell you how I got here. I thought education, knowledge and wisdom would help me get ahead in life. So I studied like mad in high school and wheeled and dealed my way into the best colleges and universities my parents couldn't afford.

Since undergraduate degrees are plentiful and no guarantee of a mega–buck salary with a major corporation, I reasoned that I had better keep going with my education. To that end I worked more years to get an M.A., M.S., M.B.A., Ph.D ... ad infinitum.

I thought that once I was well educated at all these prestigious schools, I would have business offers from all over. I felt sure that with my education the rest of my life would be easy—expensive car, gorgeous wife, big home in the suburbs in the best neighborhood, and 2.4 perfect children.

Instead of happiness, contentment, success and fulfillment, all I found was emptiness. The whole thing was meaningless.

If education wasn't the key to fulfillment, I surmised, maybe having fun was the thing to do. If I could find meaning for my life, it would be worth it all. Even if it killed me.

I joined the sexual revolution to experience all I could, but I never found any real emotional fulfillment. Most of the people I used to party with are emotionally and physically scarred and warped in their own ways. A few have died from AIDS. I have known many one–night relationships but never one person who truly loved me.

Next I tried recreation and leisure. I took up tennis, racquetball, hang gliding, sailing, scuba diving and even bungee jumping from tall bridges. Unfortunately, I had to work more hours to afford to do all these fun things. Any more fun would probably have killed me.

TV and music didn't cheer me either, for all I saw was a reflection of the sadness and emptiness of my life. I drank heavily and experimented with drugs to find a reason for living.

I tried great projects to keep me busy and to direct my creative energies. I restored a country farmhouse, but I never lived there to enjoy the peace and quiet. I bought and refurbished a loft in the city that was the envy of every real estate and decorating firm in the state. None of it made me happy or content. All these monuments to my quest for meaning left me tired, empty and alone.

People think that I have everything anyone could ever want or imagine. Sadly, I don't know what to do with it, for it means nothing.

Even with credit—nearly unlimited credit—the bills still had to be paid on time. So I worked, and worked hard. I gave myself to my vocation without reservation, hoping that I might find some sense of accomplishment and meaning. I worked miserably long hours, taking jobs no one else would touch to cut big, important deals for the company. My plan was to stay ahead of my coworkers and competition so that one day I might inherit the business and become even more wealthy and powerful.

I did inherit the business. To my dismay and despair, I am the boss doing a job that I hate. I hate getting up in the morning. I hate going to the office. I hate the staff, and I'm sure they hate me. All of the things that seemed so bright, promising and challenging are boring routine.

Why couldn't I do something useful with my life where I could find some enjoyment and satisfaction? Even if I were a farmer or a welder or a truck driver or a Maytag repairman, at least I would be doing something measurable and responsible with my own hands. At least in this way I could make a positive contribution to the world.

All this time I allowed the work that gave me some identity to rob me of the most important things in life. I missed most of my kids' birthdays, and now they are grown and gone and want nothing to do with their absentee, big-shot father. I haven't taken a restful vacation with my family in years. I have been married more than several times and am still alone. At least I have my company, my money, my big fleet of chauffeur-driven cars and people who call me sir. Still, it's all meaningless.

Here I am in the "forty something" crowd knowing that I won't live forever. I have taken pretty good care of the parts that show on the outside, with perfect caps for my teeth, hair transplants for my head, gold chains galore, liposuction and face lifts and fancy $4,000 suits from the most exclusive tailors. On the negative side of conspicuous ownership, I also have an ulcer, high blood pressure, insomnia and serious periodic bouts with nearly suicidal depression. If I keep this up I'll be dead long before I reach "fifty something."

If I do survive, what do I have to look forward to? Alzheimer's, cancer, stroke—ending my days in a nursing home with a bunch of old Yuppie relics like me named Skip, Brian, Kandi and Ashley?

One day not too far off, I'll be dead and who will mourn me? I'll be dead and gone and somebody else will enjoy my wealth. Most likely it will be one of my partners or one of my feuding kids.

I often wonder how the world will be able to get along without me. They did it for thousands of years, so I guess they will manage somehow. What bothers me most about all this death business is that I have existed all this time and done all these things and experienced everything imaginable, without ever having lived. I have gone through it all without any sense of purpose or meaning. At the end of it all I'll probably die unloved and unmourned.

I wish I had listened to my mom and dad and clung to some of the simple things from my youth. They lived well without being ostentatious about it. As I recall they loved each other and derived a sense of joy from being alive. I especially envy their special relationship with God. How I wish I could remember the things they tried to teach me. It was all so simple, and I forgot it in spite of my fancy education. God loved me, and I knew it and I felt it too.

I miss the warmth and security of being a kid to the point that I'd gladly trade dinner at the fancy French restaurant and the bottle of outrageously expensive Dom Perignon champagne for one taste of my mom's home cooking.

Don't make the same mistake that I did. All of the things I learned as an adult—how to be a big-shot and a wealthy, wise, powerful leader—don't amount to a hill of beans when compared to the simple things of God. Get to know God and His love when you are young and stay with it. That will be the only thing that will save your life and your soul.

Now this is the bottom line—I'm good at the bottom line—fear, love and trust God. Keep His commands with joy and obedient faith. You will be wiser and wealthier in things of true value than I ever was. Love the Lord and keep His commands, for everything else is meaningless and empty.

With a hope that you don't make my mistake, in love,

Solomon
King of Israel
The Ultimate Yuppie

The Shortstop's Lunch

"Jesus then took the loaves, gave thanks, and distributed to those who were seated as much as they wanted" (John 6:11).

The day of the big game was finally here. It was a terrific day for baseball, but then again, any day was a terrific day for baseball as far as I was concerned. I put on my uniform, grabbed my glove and ball and bolted for the front door. Just as I reached the end of the hallway my mom yelled, "Be home on time for supper young man, and don't forget your lunch."

"I won't mom," I replied, as I blasted open the screen door.

"Spike ... don't slam the door!"

I heard the warning but not in time to avoid the sudden crash of the door.

"Sorry mom. I forgot," I feebly apologized as I raced down the street to meet my friends for the big game. "Wish me luck."

As I headed out to the ball park, I took a peek in the bag to see what goodies my mother had packed for me to eat. I don't know what makes mothers so considerate. Although it was not a full course meal, it was enough to keep me going until supper. There in the wrinkled paper bag was one peanut butter and jelly sandwich, a couple of cookies and a banana.

I was so excited that I could hardly stand the wait until game time. I was the starting shortstop for the Galilee Giants, and today we were playing the Jericho Jaguars. This was no pick–up game with a bunch of little kids on a vacant lot. We had a regulation ball park with fences, dugouts, a flat infield and real bases. It was a nice change from the vacant lot we usually used filled with rocks, holes, broken glass and beer bottles. In fact the field was so nice that we took up a collection to get a permit so the big kids couldn't run us off.

In just a few minutes the baseball battle would begin—Giants vs. Jaguars for the make–believe World Series. All we needed was for Vin Scully to do the play–by–play.

But I was not at all prepared for the sight I beheld when I made it up the hill to the ball park. There must have been close to 5,000 people standing on our field.

"Hey! You can't stay here!" I screamed. "We have a ball game in just a few minutes!"

Good grief! There were so many people all over the field. There was a lady on second base—I mean she was sitting *on* second base! How could I turn a double play with her in the way? Boy, I had never been so mad in all my life.

"You have to go. We have a permit for this field."

I fished around in my pockets among the assorted treasures that little boys carry to find that precious official document that would establish our legal claim to the ball field. We had official permission to be here and these people didn't.

But all I could do was stand there—mad enough to spit and disappointed enough to cry.

"Sorry about the field young man. I don't think you'll get in a game today," said the stranger.

"Don't you know who's here?" he asked.

"Mister, I don't really care who is here," I barked by way of reply. I remember later that I felt bad that I snapped at him, because it wasn't his fault the game was canceled.

"Son, Jesus is here. So many people were eager to hear Him teach that they couldn't find an auditorium large enough to hold them all. He's the one who has been going around teaching and preaching. He supposedly has made blind men see and lame men walk, although I have never seen it for myself. That's why I am here today. Maybe He'll do something spectacular like that. I'd love to see it, wouldn't you?"

I had heard about Jesus. He was a favorite topic at the supper table among the adults. I didn't contribute much to the conversation because they insisted that we kids should "be seen and not heard."

But I did ask the stranger, "Is He here alone or with those 12 other guys on His team?"

I was interested because I had seen Peter once and judging from the size of him, he could have been a power hitter.

"Yes son," he answered, "they are all here. But they seem to have the same problem most of the rest of us have. In my eagerness to come and hear Jesus, I forgot to pack a lunch and there aren't any restaurants around here for miles." With that he scurried off to get a good seat in the crowd.

He had really aroused my interest, and since there was no way we could play baseball, I decided to check this whole thing out for myself. I had a real advantage over the grown–ups since it is easy to maneuver through the crowd when you're 12 years old and just a little over four feet tall.

As I worked my way around the adults, I noticed one of Jesus' disciples over to one side of the crowd, where the visitors' dugout would be. I think he was the one called Philip. He paced back and forth, muttering to himself just like a major league manager.

"I don't know what Jesus expects from me," he mumbled. "He's the one who does the miracles, not me. He brings us all the way down here, knowing there's not a hamburger place within miles. And now He tells me to find food for all these people. I sure wish He had thought of that before we came all the way out here.

"I checked the treasury," he grumbled. "We've got enough money for 10 or 12 Big Macs and maybe a few bags of fries and maybe a couple sodas. But we'll never have enough to feed all of these people. We'd blow close to a whole year's pay trying to get something to eat for so many.

"I just don't know what to do. What does Jesus expect from me anyway?"

Poor old Philip was really working up to a nervous breakdown over this "feed the crowd" thing. I figured as long as I was miserable about the cancellation of the big game, I'd unload some of that on him.

"It serves you right not to have any food," I taunted. "We had a game here until you guys came and ruined all our plans." I was all set to pile on the misery when I felt a gentle tap on my shoulder.

"Be fair. It's not Philip's fault the game was canceled. Sometimes even the pros get rained out or postponed. I'm sure you can get the guys back to play tomorrow when we have all gone."

I turned and recognized the man as Andrew, another of Jesus' disciples. He was Peter's brother. He wasn't as big as Peter, but he was friendlier than the rest of them. What amazed me was that while all the other adults were doing grown–up stuff, he was spending his time talking to a kid like me. He made me feel as if I were important, and I liked the way it felt.

"Philip has a tough assignment," Andrew continued. "I think Jesus knew there would be no food. My guess is that Jesus wanted to test Philip's faith, like He does sometimes to see if we've grown enough to trust Him to be true to His word.

"Test or no test, though," Andrew said, "I'm getting a bit hungry myself.

I hope Philip finds something soon."

Andrew swept his arm to show the vast expanse before us. "Take a look around. Would you believe not one grown–up had the good sense to pack something to eat? We were all so eager to hear Jesus that we didn't even pack a candy bar or a piece of fruit."

In all of the excitement, I had forgotten about the little lunch my mother had packed for me.

"Mr. Andrew, if you promise not to laugh, I have some food you could have. My mom packed a little snack. It isn't much, but you are welcome to it. Maybe you could give it to Jesus 'cause He'll be pretty hungry before the day is out. It isn't much, but it's all I have."

His gentle manner assured me right from the start that he wouldn't make fun of me.

"Of course I won't laugh," he said. "I'm proud of you for being so willing to share with others even if it means giving up your own lunch. In fact, I'm certain that Jesus can do something unique with it. Would you like to meet Him?"

"Are you kidding," I stammered. I almost said, "does a duck have lips?" but I figured I had better not be a wise guy around such nice people.

It was great. Imagine a kid like me having the opportunity to meet Jesus of Nazareth up close and personal! It was better than box seats at the World Series. In fact, I told Andrew that I would give anything to meet Jesus— even my prized baseball card collection.

Soon after, we worked our way to the other side of the crowd so we could see Jesus. He wasn't especially good–looking or rugged like Peter. He did have powerful hands though. It must have come from all the years working in the family carpentry shop.

I had worked out what I was going to say when I met Him. I'd tell Him how nice it was to meet Him but that I didn't appreciate having all these people on our ball field.

"Jesus," said Andrew, "this is Spike, the young man I was telling You about. He was the only one with enough wisdom to bring some food. He wanted to meet You and to give his lunch to You."

As soon as Jesus turned to look at me, all the smart speeches vanished from my mind.

"Hello sir. I have heard quite a lot about You. I feel honored to meet You."

Jesus turned in His seat so that we were face to face, only inches apart. He wanted to get close enough so that I would know our conversation was important enough not to be interrupted by grown–up business.

"Andrew tells me that you want Me to have your lunch. He even said that you would be willing to give up your baseball card collection just to meet Me. They are your greatest treasures, aren't they?"

All I could muster by way of a reply was a weak, "Yes, sir."

"I am the one who feels honored because you have placed such a high value on our meeting. Your mother must love you very much to have taken the time to make sure you have enough to eat."

Remembering why I was here, I pulled the battered bag from behind my back and dumped out its contents. "Let's see—one peanut butter and jelly sandwich, one banana and a couple of my mom's great chocolate chip cookies."

Jesus' gentle yet powerful manner made me feel loved and accepted. And those eyes—they seemed to look right through me.

"Spike, I know how much you were looking forward to your game today. I know that you are hurt and a bit angry. But these people have come here today to have their lives changed. That's important, isn't it?"

Jesus knew exactly how I felt. Yet He never talked down to me or rushed on to take care of other things.

"It's no problem, Jesus. I feel better already, and we can always play tomorrow. My dad says You are a great prophet sent from God. My Uncle Vinnie says that You have incredible powers to heal. Uncle Joe, the hard–head of the family, says You are a phony. He thinks everyone has an angle and is out to make a fast buck at someone else's expense. But I know who You are. You can't kid a kid. You really are the Son of God just like You said. That's why I want You to take my lunch. It isn't much, but I know You can do something special with it. I think if You wanted to, You could feed this whole mob with just my little lunch."

I looked to the side and could see that the disciples were getting a bit impatient, and I knew that our meeting would soon be over.

Before I could speak again Jesus looked deeply into my eyes and called me by my given name that only the family knew.

"Arnold—I know you don't like that name and prefer Spike better, so that will be our little secret—I will always treasure this meeting. I appreciate your thoughtfulness, and I want you to know that no matter what happens and no matter what you hear, I'll never forget you."

"Jesus, I'll never forget You either."

As I turned to walk away, I knew He would do something miraculous with my little bag lunch. He made me feel important and happy beyond anything I had ever experienced, and I just had to let Him know that I'd be there to do something for Him again.

"Hey Jesus," I shouted across the widening distance, "when I come back tomorrow I'll hit a homer for You."

Jesus smiled and waved back as if He knew that was exactly what would happen.

"Help! I've Fallen and ..."

"As the Philistines moved closer to attack him, David quickly ran to the battle line to meet him. Reaching into his bag and taking out a stone, he slung it and struck the Philistine on the forehead. The stone sank into his forehead and he fell face down on the ground. So David triumphed over the Philistine with a sling and a stone; without a sword in his hand he struck down the Philistine and killed him. When the Philistines saw that their hero was dead, they turned and ran" (1 Sam. 17:48–51).

We know how David came to a battle site to deliver lunch to his older brothers who were serving in the Israeli military and how he heard Goliath, the Philistine, ridiculing the army of the Lord. Any kid can tell you how he defeated the giant armed with a shepherd's sling and five smooth stones rather than using King Saul's armor and weapons. David proved the Lord was in charge and would fight the battle for David and deliver the warrior–giant into the hands of a humble shepherd boy.

But what about the giant? What was his reaction to all of this? What might have been going through his mind as this kid came out to face him in mortal combat? I imagine it was similar to General Custer when he attacked what he thought was a small concentration of Indians and understood he was not going to get away this time!

We will never know for certain about Goliath's attitude that day, although it might be interesting to see how the story unfolds as he might tell it. Imagine you are there to witness the duel from the giant's point of view.

I enjoy being huge. Sure it's hard finding clothes and shoes to fit and occasionally I feel a bit of a freak, but now that I am a well–paid champion of the Philistine army, things are working out fine.

No more "How's the weather up there?" cracks. When I go out people call me sir and step aside as I pass. Nobody messes with Goliath. I'm bad, I'm mean and I'm tough.

I have had a ball getting my own way because who is going to argue with a dude like me who is 10 feet tall? I can do as I please since none of those little guys are brave enough or stupid enough to tangle with me. The last one who tried got busted up real bad! That one Israeli soldier did fairly well against me. In fact, I rather enjoyed hearing him whimper and grovel and beg for mercy before I finally killed him.

This army of Jehovah ain't much—a bunch of snivelling cowards. Even their King Saul sits in his tent and shivers with fright whenever I come on the scene. That's why I go out each day to the valley to taunt them and make fun of their king, their puny country and their God. For me, killing Hebrews in hand–to–hand combat is about as dangerous as checkers!

"Hey, any of you have the stomach for a little fight? Why don't you send one of your brave jellyfish out to fight me hand–to–hand, right here ... right now. You'll all die anyway once our army rolls into high gear. Let's just have some fun, and I promise to get it over with quickly.

"So who will it be? C'mon ... who will be a man and face me?"

Old Goliath was very confident of his prowess as a warrior—so much so that he must have nearly had a stroke when little David answered his challenge in a showdown to the death.

"What is this coming out to face me? You must be kidding! Is this your idea of a joke? He's nothing but a runt of a kid! What do think I am? Is this the best your God has to offer? I'm going to make you wish you had never been born."

After I toss him around a bit, I'll rip off an arm or a leg because they really made me mad sending out a mouthy kid spouting off about how his God is going to beat me and the Philistine army. I should break off his head and leave him in the sand for the buzzards just to teach them a lesson.

Now what is that brat doing? Picking up stones? He should be looking for a good place to hide.

What's that again ... a stone for me and one each for my four ugly brothers? Now I'm really mad!! I'll fix that little creep!!

"Kid—knock off the speeches. You should have run while you had the chance."

You know, he moves pretty well for a kid—light on his feet and good reflexes. He'll tire and be easy for me to run through with my spear.

"Hold still, kid, and I'll make this quick and efficient. You have put up a better show for the others in your Lord's army."

This should be easy. Man, this kid really believes all that stuff about his conquering Lord. Sure hope there is nothing to it because I'd hate to be beaten by a kid. A rival warrior would be bad enough—but a kid, no way. Then I'd really have to bust some heads to get even.

Hasn't he got the sense he was born with? He wants to fight in close. Well, if that's how he wants to die, so be it.

Isn't that cute. He's going to shoot me with a rock. I have enough armor plate on me that I could deflect a spear—and he's shooting rocks. He'd have to be one fabulous marksman to make a shot that would hurt me. I'm Goliath. I'm a champion. I'm tough and invincible. He couldn't possibly get off a shot that goooooooooooood ...

Oh no. He hit me in the forehead just below my helmet. I can't believe it. What is that? Blood ... *my* blood? Oh my aching head! I can't believe he made that shot. I just can't. It's impossible.

Maybe his God is God after all. But what would the Philistines say? They look up to me ... I'm their leader ... their hero ... their idol. I can barely stand ... the whole valley is getting fuzzy ... I can hardly see ... this can't be happening ... I can't see ... I can't be dying—not Goliath ... not me.

Where is that kid? At least I can take him with me ... but I can't move my arms ... I can't find my sword ... the ground is swirling and I can hardly see. I can't stand ... this can't be death ... not me ... it's not fair ... I'm Goliath!

Paul shares some good advice for other giants who think they are big enough to get their own way without having the Lord part of their lives. He speaks of feeling that we are above temptation and that we could never be defeated by the influence of sin in our lives much the same way Goliath felt about his skill in battle against David. In 1 Corinthians 10:12 Paul writes, "So, if you think you are standing firm, be careful that you don't fall!"

Just about the time you think you have it together to the point that you no longer need God in your life and that you are wealthy, happy, lucky and nearly invincible—remember the Philistine giant face down in the dust.

Long Ago ... in a Country Far, Far Away ...

"After Jesus was born in Bethlehem in Judea ... Magi from the east came to Jerusalem and asked, 'Where is the One who has been born king of the Jews? We saw His star in the east and have come to worship Him.'" (Matt. 2:1–2).

Have we heard the Christmas story so often that it has lost its sense of wonder and excitement? Has it become too comfortable and predictable? Yet it was the anticipation of the Savior's birth that gave people hope for thousands of years. Perhaps we have been spoiled by film makers such as George Lucas and Steven Spielberg and only get excited about the adventures of the characters from the Star Wars saga. If we use some imagination, it would not be too difficult to make the Magi from the Christmas story into the wise men from Star Wars—the Jedi.

Those were evil days back then, with Israel in the hands of the Empire that stretched from Anglia to the Indus River under the sandalled heels of Rome's Imperial troopers. For the Hebrews, the promise of a Savior–king gave hope.

"Long ago ... in a country far, far away" after Jesus was born in Bethlehem in Judea, Jedi from the east came to Jerusalem and asked, "Where is the One who has been born King of the Jews? We saw His star in the east and have come to worship Him" (Matt. 2:2).

These were not aged seers but warrior–defenders of goodness and truth, champions of life and justice, seeking the One who was to be the Way, the Truth and the Life. They served in the tradition of Joshua, Caleb and Nehemiah before the evil days of idolatry and the conquest of the Empire.

When Herod Vader received news of the Jedi's presence in the city, he was greatly disturbed. He called together all the chief priests and teachers of the law and asked them where the Christ was to be born. "You, Bethlehem, in the land of Judah, are by no means the least among the rulers of Judah; for out of you will come a ruler who will be the shepherd of My people Israel" (Matt. 2:6) was the reply.

"Why was I not informed of this prophecy?" he demanded.

"Herod Vader, we assumed that you knew," his advisor stated, cowering in fear. "It is a common prophecy we have heard for generations."

"Let us find this new king and crush this rebellion against my authority."

Herod Vader, an imposing figure in a flowing, floor–length black cape, carried himself as one accustomed to being obeyed without question.

"Gentlemen," he said to the Jedi in a deep voice that seemed to reverberate from the depths of hell, "Thank you for coming to inform us of the arrival of this new king. Please, friends, bring me news of this king so I may go and worship Him also."

Lies—all lies. Herod Vader never worshipped anyone or anything. As soon as the Jedi had departed, Herod Vader called his inner circle of sages and advisors to the throne room.

"Go now. Keep the gold, frankincense and myrrh, but bring the child to me. You have failed me for the last time!"

Well aware of the danger, the Jedi followed the star and found the child just as it had been foretold. Filled with joy they worshipped Him—the one who had come into the world to bring sinful people back into a right relationship with God. They had a real sense of wonder and amazement being in the presence of the Son of God—a sense we may have lost over time.

Being warned of Herod Vader's treachery, the Jedi returned to their own country by a different route. I would not have wanted to be the one to deliver the news to Herod Vader that they had not located the child and that the Jedi had escaped.

But we don't need a movie version of the story to inspire us. What we need is a willing heart seeking Christ's forgiveness and love to make the adventure tangible and personal as the Lord changes us. Catch the thrill as you begin your own adventure in Jesus Christ. We can save the duels with light–sabers for another time.

Showdown at Rahab's Place

"Then Joshua son of Nun secretly sent two spies from Shittim. 'Go, look over the land,' he said, 'especially Jericho.' So they went and entered the house of ... Rahab and stayed there" (Josh. 2:1).

Let your imagination run, and try to see events as they might have been if the story of the siege of Jericho came from the American west rather than from ancient Israel.

Jericho was much like any other wide–open town on the Canaan frontier—except for the wall that circled the city. Maybe it was there to keep the law out and the bad guys in, or vice versa. As a popular place for mule skinners, snake oil salesmen, ranchers, dance hall girls and anyone else eager to make a fast buck, it catered to all manner of people of high and low estate—mostly low. Jericho was located on one of the major cattle trails from Egypt to Assyria, and like any number of places like it—Tombstone, Deadwood, Dodge, Abilene—it was big, boisterous and dangerous, with the only law being the law of the gun—shoot fast and shoot straight, or die.

One day two strangers rode into Jericho and went straight to Miss Rahab's Place, because it was the social and cultural hub of the city. Miss Rahab ran a saloon and dance hall where a mule skinner or cowboy could get a cool drink after a long trip to settle the dust a bit. There, too, cowpokes might get a bath, a shave and maybe drink, relax and regale each other with tall tales of their adventures.

Miss Rahab runs her establishment much like the Alhambra in Tombstone or the Long Branch in Dodge City, with a piano player, a high stakes poker game or two and people drinking. Once in a while someone gets liquored up and raises a ruckus. But Miss Rahab doesn't take to violence or bad manners, so she throws them out as quickly as possible.

The law, such as it is, isn't much help since they have no one with the ability or character of a Wyatt Earp, Bat Masterson or Bill Tilghman of the Texas Rangers. Most of Jericho's so-called peace officers are more concerned about getting a "piece of the action" rather than in actually keeping the peace and public safety.

Into this maelstrom of rowdy activity the two strangers came.

"Howdy gents," said the bartender as they bellied up to the long polished bar with the gleaming brass foot rail in the only decent establishment in town. "What's your pleasure?"

"Just a cold glass of water, a good, thick steak and some peace and quiet."

That should have been the first indication that something was unusual about these two, since the only drink they regularly served at Miss Rahab's was rot-gut whiskey. Sometimes called "pop skull" or "who hit John," it was cheap and powerful. One long slug of that noxious brew could often numb a man's tongue as well as his brain, getting a person roaring drunk for just a little money. Good thing too, because by the time the card sharks and swindlers got through, a little money was all most had left. Some even used the emergency stash cowboys kept in the empty cylinder of their revolvers that served to make sure the hammer did not rest on a live round so they wouldn't accidentally shoot off a toe. Also, it was nice to have a few dollars put aside in case they needed doctoring or burying far from home.

"Gonna be here in Jericho long?" the bar keep queried, trying to be hospitable. "Business or pleasure?"

"No, we are farmers from far away. We're looking for a little property we can pick up and call our own," the taller stranger replied. Technically it wasn't a lie since he and his partner knew they were there to scout out the city and see how best to take it over ... by force if necessary.

"Farmers you say? Well, welcome to Jericho, and may your stay be profitable and pleasant. And good luck—you are going to need it. This is a tough town, especially for strangers."

The two were dressed like farmers and talked the jargon of crops, rainfall and grain prices. But something was not quite right about these two. One was well over six feet tall, rangy and tough as saddle leather. He was the spokesman. His counterpart was a stocky man of about 5'10" with muscles that bulged even beneath his loose-fitting shirt. Although he never said it aloud, it was like the second man was always ready to address the tall one as "sir" or "captain."

They did not carry themselves like farmers. The clothes were right, but the manner was wrong. Their hands were not gnarled and broken from years of tilling the soil. Nor did they did have the "poor me" downtrodden look of "sod busters." On the contrary, these two carried themselves with an air of self–assurance, knowing they could handle themselves in any situation regardless of how violent. They were hard men, and had anyone taken notice, they were memorizing every detail.

Their eyes swept the room and carefully recorded everything—each exit, each armed guard, each staircase. They took special notice of the sawed–off 12–gauge shotgun kept on the counter behind the bar.

Like everyone else on the Jericho frontier, they were armed. It was a dangerous place to be, with snakes, bandits, poisonous lizards and a huge band of former Hebrew slaves roaming loose. Word was that the Hebrews had already laid to waste every town they passed in their search for land, lurking somewhere out on the plains not too far from Jericho itself. And there were those out on the frontier who would kill you for your money, for your boots or just for fun.

Those who rarely draw their gun other than to shoot a snake or some meat for the table, carry the pistol high on the belt so it's not in the way of their wagon or plow. These two carried theirs in well–worn holsters, slung low on the hip and tied down at the thigh like a gunfighter. One might guess that they may have been gunfighters, ex–military or maybe even mercenaries. In any case, they acted like they knew what to do with their weapons and would be ready to use them with deadly efficiency. That and the razor–sharp "Arkansas toothpick" with the 12–inch blade the captain had on his belt should have been a definite tip–off that they were not what they claimed to be.

Unlike other desperadoes of the day, they did not arouse any wariness as to their mission. People remembered the sight of Cole and Bob Younger and Frank and Jesse James and the gang riding into Northfield, Minnesota to rob the First National Bank. But the two strangers didn't look like that.

All of those outlaw types were fairly easy to spot in their linen "duster" trail overcoats and fine horses—and because they were usually silent and surly too. These two were just asking questions like "When do they close the city gate at night?" or "How many men are in the local militia garrison?" or "What information do you have about the Hebrews from Egypt?" They were friendly without being overly familiar in probing for specific information about the city. But they were more than just interested— they were there on a reconnaissance mission.

Most didn't notice these two strangers and went about their daily routines. But Bart Jenkins, one of the sheriff's deputies, looked at them warily. He was almost as corrupt as Sheriff "Big Jim" Moody himself.

Bart fancied himself to be a talented gunman, since he had killed eight men along the way. He took great pride in showing off his fancy, engraved Army Colt .45 pistols as if he was Billy the Kid himself. But deep down, Bart was a coward of the worst sort. All of the men he killed were either unarmed, old and defenseless or shot in the back. If he ever had to face a fast draw in a fair fight, he would probably panic and faint.

Bart sauntered over to where the two were eating dinner and initiated a conversation loud enough for the whole room to hear, "Hey gents, we keep an eye on strangers here in Jericho these days. Planning on staying long?"

"Depends," one of the strangers replied softly.

"Depends on what?" Bart pressed, eager to intimidate the newcomers.

"Depends on whether we find out what we need to know or not."

By now the deputy was aware that these two were definitely not farmers and not impressed or threatened by his show of authority. Trying a different line of questioning, the deputy backed up and tried again. "Didn't catch the name, stranger."

"Didn't throw it," came the curt, chilling reply.

Feeling impotent in his inability to push the two "farmers," Bart started to reach for his sidearm. That threat had always worked on farmers before. But in less time than it takes to blink, the tall stranger nearest him drew his long-barrelled Walker Colt and cocked and pressed it to the deputy's nose.

All Bart could do was listen quietly—or risk having his nose and most of his face splattered across the bar's back wall. Sweating profusely, he concentrated on the stranger's words while staring down the cavernous bore of the huge pistol.

Quite certain that he had his undivided attention, one of the strangers told Bart, "I'll say this quietly, and I'll say it once. We are leaving and we don't want to be disturbed. We have come to have a look around, and we will be on our way as soon as we are finished.

"We can do this the easy way, or we can do it the hard way. It doesn't matter to us. You can go straight up or draped over the saddle—your choice. Do you understand?"

Bart nodded sheepishly and with that was released—shaking uncontrollably with both fear and rage.

The two quietly exited into the alley in back of Miss Rahab's, and just as quickly Bart was on his way to tell his boss about these two dangerous men. They were fast with a gun and too tough for him to handle. Surely they must be here as spies or outlaws, and nothing good for Jericho or the sheriff would come of it.

It didn't take long for the sheriff to get a posse of his equally corrupt cronies to try to track down the two strangers. They headed to Miss Rahab's place since that is where Bart had his nearly fatal encounter with them.

Rahab had been quietly observing the strangers and noted something odd about the way they carried themselves and their proficiency with firearms. She knew they were committed to whatever mission brought them to town and that they were dangerous.

So Rahab had several choices. She could turn the spies in for a reward; say nothing and take her chances in a gun battle with the sheriff and his men; or hide the two and hope they could spare her and her family when the inevitable fight finally erupted. She knew that the Jericho thugs were no match for these two fighting men or their confederates who might be lurking up in the hills.

Making her decision in seconds, Rahab chose to do her part to save her family and herself.

She heard the wicked sheriff down the street yelling instructions to his lackeys, "Let's get these two. Joe, you and Bart go over to the livery and get a rope 'cause if we find them, we're gonna string 'em up right here in front of town hall at high noon! The buzzards will be eatin' their carcasses by nightfall! So get with it!"

Rahab rushed out into the narrow alley behind the saloon to warn the two strangers about the sheriff. They had completed their reconnaissance and were discussing their options—hide, run or shoot it out.

"I don't know who you are, and you may or may not decide to trust me, but the sheriff is getting up a posse to find you. If he gets you he'll kill you for sure." She continued, "We don't have much time. If you trust me, I know someplace where I can hide you until you can get out of town. But whatever you do, you had better make up your minds right now 'cause the sheriff is just down the street."

The two gave each other a look that spoke volumes. When you live on the run in a hostile country, you learn to evaluate people based on little more than a facial expression or a tone of voice. Rahab seemed honest, and they would have to trust her with their lives. They would have no

hesitation about facing down the sheriff and his men in a running gun battle if necessary, but they knew the importance of the mission and needed
to make sure they got back to camp with the information on Jericho. Their
job was to scout out the place, not to shoot it out like the OK Corral.

"Thank you, ma'am," the captain replied. "We are much obliged for
your help. Lead the way."

"If I betray them," Rahab thought, "the last sight I'll probably see will be
the lightning–fast draw of the tall stranger's .44." But no word was spoken
in that regard as she took them up the outside back stairs to the attic store
room where some freshly skinned hides were drying to be made into
leather.

The smell was dreadful! "Terrible" hardly even comes close in describing
the stench. But they carefully noted that there was a small window from the
upper storeroom that led to the wall and out to freedom. It would not be
easy, but a man in good condition could squeeze through the little window
and lower himself to safety outside the city.

"Stay here. If you hear them coming up the stairs, hide under the skins.
Don't make a sound. All we can hope is that they won't like the smell and
will leave. I'll do my best to cover for you. Trust me." And with that she left.

"I guess we don't have much choice except to trust her. I recall from my
folks, that is what Aaron and some of the others said—'trust me.' That is
why we're here in Jericho now ... 40 years behind schedule."

"You're right," the captain replied. "But did you notice she never asked
about a reward? If they know who we are and why we are here, there
should be a pretty hefty reward for us—dead or alive. She could turn us in,
pocket the money and be a hero all in the same day."

"It seems a shame that after she has been so good to us, she and all her
family will be killed once Joshua and the rest get here. When the shooting
starts they won't be able to tell friend from foe. Maybe we can help her."

"Let's get out of one mess before we start another one, okay?"

A few minutes passed before they heard angry shouting from the saloon
below.

"Where are they, Rahab? Bring out those two strangers who said they
were farmers. Don't lie to me, girl. One of my deputies saw them come in
here a while back. If they are farmers, then I'm Queen Cleopatra of the
Nile! Those two are spies from those dad–blamed Hebrews we've been
hearing about. Bunch of rotten sheepherders—all of them."

"Yeah, boss. The tall one's real quick with a gun too. Like to near blow my head clean off if I hadn't beat him to the draw and run to get you." Bart never could resist embellishing a good yarn to make himself to be the hero of the story.

"You keep still! If you were so all–fired good with a gun, they'd be on their way to Doc Miller's or Boot Hill by now. You're just lucky I don't plug you right here myself for being a stupid, gutless coward."

"Rahab," the sheriff continued, "I'm waiting. And I'm gettin' tired, so don't try anything funny. Bring those boys out here right smart and things will go well with you—or would you rather have me take this place apart piece by piece?

"I'm losin' my patience, girl. They saw those two in your place just a few minutes before we came. And no one came past us."

Scratching his rather portly middle, the sheriff went on with his interrogation. "Don't you have a storeroom or somethin' up at the top of those back stairs? Let's us go take a look–see. My brother holds the mortgage on this place, and it wouldn't go well for you or your kin if we were to find out that you were hiding those two varmints."

Rahab was not the sort of person to either go back on her word or to take abuse from anyone in her own establishment—including the law. A notable character trait, since had anyone been able to see under the piles of foul-smelling hides, two heavily armed men with guns cocked were ready for anything. If there was to be gunplay, Rahab might get hit in the cross fire, right after the first two shots took care of the sheriff and his lackey.

"Dag gonnit Rahab, what's that smell? Did something crawl in here and die?"

"No, you immense idiot," Rahab shouted, breaking her silence and taking the offensive. "Those are hides drying so we can tan them and make shoes and things. Don't you know anything—or are you as dumb as you look?" She was concerned for her family but was not overly intimidated by this so–called law officer. Maybe if she sounded put out and aggressive, they might leave without making a more careful inspection.

"If I hear you know where those two boys are and you're holdin' out on me, I'll be back and it won't be pleasant. So for the last time, tell me everything you know about them."

"Well sheriff, the boys at the bar heard the two strangers talking about leaving with the pack train of the Lazy J cattle drive. As far as I know they were headed that way toward Crescent Moon Pass to the ford of the Jordan by Abdullah's Flats. If you quit jawin' at me and move fast, you may be able to catch them there by first light."

"You heard the lady. Get saddled up. A bonus to the man that brings them in—dead or alive. Now, let's ride."

With that the entire bunch ran to the street and with great confusion and clatter, mounted up and rode off to Abdullah's Flats ... in the wrong direction.

As soon as it was clear that there was no immediate danger except from maybe one of the sheriff's goons left behind to keep an eye on Rahab's place, she ran to the storeroom to check on her guests.

"It's all clear. They've gone. You can come out now."

She was relieved to see that they were all right. But her elation was nothing compared to theirs in being liberated from their foul-smelling concealment.

"You boys need to be on your way, but it's not safe to go out through town. I can lower a rope through that window to let you down just outside the wall."

"But before you go, I want to ask something," she began. "I have heard the news of your people and I know that things are going to get pretty hot around here once your friends catch up with you. I'm not worried for me so much, but when the shooting starts, I need to make sure my family is all right."

"Miss Rahab, you said to trust you, and we did, and you were true to your word. So we'll make you a deal—no, a promise," said the captain. "When the fighting starts, there will be plenty of smoke and noise and people running all over. Once it gets serious, there's no way to go looking for people inside the town. So, when it happens, make sure your family is up here in this room with you. Hang that red-colored lariat out the same window we're leavin' from, and we'll make sure you're kept safe. It is only fair; you saved our lives, and we'll save yours."

The other man chimed in an additional word of warning. "If you don't follow this plan and don't have the rope where we can find it, or if you are taken outside this room, we can't promise anything. You'll be caught in the flying lead just like the rest. But if you do what we have said, we give you our word that you will get out safely and that you and your family will be treated kindly."

Rahab nodded her assent and felt an unexplained sense of assurance that she could trust these two dangerous men with her life and that of her family.

She helped them climb out the window and watched as they slid silently down the wall and off into the night. She thought to herself that the sheriff would not want to meet up with those two in the dark. She probably saved his life for the moment by sending him on a wild pursuit in the wrong direction.

It didn't take long before the two strangers made it back to their camp and reported their findings to their leaders. It was one thing riding into a small town with guns blazing behind a herd of stampeding longhorns but quite another finding a way to get into a walled city. The defenders could shoot from safety while you were exposed. Something special was required if they were to pull this one off.

The plan of attack was nothing if not novel. The entire band was to march around the city wall at the same time each day just out of range of the defenders. The oddest part was that it was to be done in complete silence—no shouting threats or firing guns into the air.

Many had seen firsthand Indian and outlaw attacks before. The yelling was almost as terrifying as the high–pitched whine of bullets passing close at hand or the whoosh of an arrow in flight.

It was only after they had made the trip around the city in silence for six days that they would sound the charge and rush to the attack.

Meanwhile back in Jericho, the sheriff returned from his fool's errand at Abdullah's Flats and points beyond. You could tell it was an election year as he blustered and bragged of how he single–handedly drove those two strangers out of town and tracked them night and day, saving the poor townspeople by his personal courage. He talked as if he had just brought in Jesse James, Billy the Kid and the Hole in the Wall Gang, all by himself.

The people stood around with rapt attention as he regaled them with harrowing tales of blazing guns, desperate shoot–outs and narrow escapes. The gullible townspeople were impressed, all but Rahab, who knew that the sheriff could not have possibly accomplished any of this by going in the wrong direction. Had he actually met up with the two well–armed strangers, the sheriff would be food for vultures somewhere out on the prairie, dead from lead poisoning—of the .45 caliber variety.

Bart backed up the lie and was quite vocal in his telling of his own personal adventures—until he saw Rahab watching from the edge of the crowd. His little brain remembered the terror and the shame of his first encounter with the strangers. He was sure that Rahab was involved somehow. He may not have been smart, but he was dangerous, especially when he was backed into a corner like a wounded animal.

Early in the morning when the sun had just risen over the top of Jacob's Mesa, the strangers and their entire army gathered in front of Jericho. It didn't take a military genius to understand their intentions. They were heavily armed and obviously not there to see the sights.

The mayor of Jericho was spineless and lacked any real character. He ran the general store and as long as he could charge outrageous prices and feed his greed from the work of others, he was content to allow the sheriff and his cronies free reign in the city. He was the sort of man who would smile and be gracious when talking face to face but would not hesitate to shoot a man in the back.

As the duly elected (albeit rigged) official for the citizenry of Jericho, he had the task of determining the intentions of this band of armed men amassing in front of the city.

"What do you fellers want?" he asked, trying hard to not to allow them to hear the fear in his voice. At least he had the wall to hide behind, and that was some comfort. "What are your intentions?"

He repeated his questions, each time asking louder and with more intensity, and each time the reply was the same—silence.

"Who are you?" he roared, desperately hoping for some sign or answer. But as before there was none.

After several minutes of shouting his questions and gaining no reply, the mayor quivered when he saw the men dismount in preparation for attack.

"Be ready on the wall, they're comin'!"

But they didn't. I am not sure what was more unnerving—having them draw weapons to begin the expected attack, or what came next.

Without saying a word, the entire army began to walk around the city in complete silence. After their initial astonishment, the men on the walls thought it very amusing and liberally jeered and taunted the army.

"Is that the best you can do? Why don't you come on ahead and face us like men, or are you a bunch of yellow–bellied cowards?"

This went on for several days. With each passing day the nerves of the defenders became more raw as fear, the sun and the prospect of imminent violence gripped their hearts. There were no more taunts, no bravado coming from the men on the wall.

Instead, there was the haunting plea yelled to the silent army outside the walls begging to know, "Who are you?"

But there was never a reply. They were about to find out.

On that last orbit around the city, each man knew his duty. The city known for corruption and lawlessness was to fall, and everyone living there along with it. All but Rahab, if she remembered the arrangement she had made with the strangers.

On that last pass around the city walls the strangest thing happened. They had gone for days in silence, but now there was a blast from the biggest trumpet section ever assembled and the entire army let out a scream which emanated from deep inside each man, calling forth the most violent and bloodcurdling cacophony imaginable. When the defenders on the wall heard it, they were paralyzed with fear.

As soon as the trumpets blew and the men shouted, the walls began to shake and crumble, leaving huge gaps in the city defenses. Dozens of armed Hebrew men poured in. People were screaming, bullets were flying and Jericho's manpower was falling on every hand. One member of the posse that had hunted the captain fell, struck by five shots at the same time.

When the captain and his aide came through the broken wall, the first person they met was Bart. The swagger was gone, replaced by abject terror, with the knowledge that death by a bullet was but a moment away and there was nothing he could do to prevent it. While he cursed the two strangers at the top of his voice, Bart's eyes showed that he wanted to make a play for his fancy revolvers but he was terrified.

Amid the din of the running gun battle with people falling, screaming, moaning and running, there was an eerie calm as the captain holstered his weapon and invited Bart to make the first move. The mayor and many of the corrupt town council, as well as most of the men in the sheriff's employ, already lay dead in the dusty street by the livery stable and in front of Miss Rahab's place.

Right to the end Bart tried to make a deal to save his miserable life. He made a move as if surrendering, but instead he made a hasty lunge for his gun. But before he could clear leather, two shots rang out from the captain's .44 and Bart lay dead in the street with two neatly punched holes in his vest. He was given a fair chance to draw and defend himself—a chance he would not have given others.

Relying on years of military training and sensing that danger was all around but as yet unseen, the captain turned quickly only to find himself under the careful aim of an enemy's weapon. He knew he could not turn and fire in time, but he had to try anyway. As he spun to face the new threat, he heard the roar of a rifle and the solid thwack of the huge bullet into the soft mass of one of the sheriff's deputies. He thought he had left his rifle in the scabbard, but his friend remembered to bring it, "just in case." In this case, it was the difference between life and death.

Some begged for their lives—other died gamely, putting up a brave if futile defense. The sheriff tried to hide but was cut down by the onrushing force even as he was preparing to shoot a man in the back; he was a coward to the very end.

It seemed like hours, but it was actually only minutes when the order to cease fire rang throughout the town. There remained sporadic gun fire as invaders rushed from house to house and building to building to crush any remaining resistance. Several heavily armed Israelite warriors made a dash for the back stairs of Rahab's place ready to shoot it out with anyone left in the establishment.

They bolted up the stairs, weapons at the ready, and kicked in the wooden door to Rahab's storeroom where just a few days earlier she had hid the spies. Rabab's 10–year–old niece screamed as she saw weapons leveled at their heads.

Fortunately the captain and his assistant made it in time to give the command "hold your fire!" for these were the people they had promised to protect. A few more seconds and Rahab and her family would have met the same fate as the rest of Jericho. But the two spies, strong men and unafraid of battle, remembered their pledge and brought Rahab and all her family from the carnage unharmed. Her faith had saved her—and her family.

II.

———— ◆ ————

Luminous Lyrics

Scripture says to "make a joyful noise unto the Lord." Sometimes we are fortunate just to be in tune, sometimes we make beautiful music and other times we just make noise. But the music of the Lord's heart always matches the need of our heart.

Sometimes the Lord gives me a simple melody that stays spooled in my head all day long, brightening my day at work and lifting my spirits when problems and difficulties arise. At other times He sends a full movie soundtrack in 70 mm Dolby surround–sound, complete with special effects.

> "Shout for joy to the Lord, all the earth,
> burst forth into jubilant song with music;
> make music to the Lord with the harp,
> with the harp and the sound of singing,
> with trumpets and the blast of the ram's horn—
> shout for joy before the Lord, the King.
> Let the sea resound, and everything in it,
> the world, and all who live in it.
> Let the rivers clap their hands,
> let the mountains sing together for joy;
> let them sing before the Lord."
>   (Ps. 98:4–9)

And He Walks
with Me

Being a Salvationist bandsman has caused a minor problem in my officership ministry. I know the tunes to most of our songs, since we accompany the singing, but I don't always know the words.

Like most bandsmen, I have heard or played our great songs of faith umpteen–thousand times, to the point where they have almost lost their impact. After so many playings, their power to move me has faded like a garment that loses its color and texture after repeated washings. The effects of this desensitizing process were brought home to me during a nursing home meeting as God the Holy Spirit once again opened my eyes with His loving correction.

We were in the assembly room—a brigade of cadets, many wheelchair–bound patients and me, the host corps officer. It was a meeting much like any other nursing home meeting—hot, and filled with the ever–present smell of antiseptic.

The cadets finished their participation, and the leader asked if anyone had a favorite hymn that we could sing as our closing song. By then we had already sung most of the classics. The suggestion was "I Come to the Garden Alone"—a song I had sung and heard hundreds of times.

The woman who requested the hymn was about 80 years old, give or take a few years, and seated in a wheelchair with both feet securely bandaged. Her hands were gnarled and swollen from the cruel ravages of arthritis. She didn't have one tooth to call her own. She was just another lady who had outlived most of her peers, and because of old age or medical circumstances, she was in this place. But she was someone's mother, sister, grandmother, wife. She had probably raised a family and in the process lived through more recorded history in her lifetime than in any other age since Adam and Eve.

I tried to reach out to her, but I couldn't understand most of what she said. I wasn't sure that anything I was saying was getting through to her. Until that song ...

And He walks with me,
and He talks with me,
and He tells me I am His own.
And the joy we share as we tarry there,
None other has ever known.

(C. Austin Miles)

God walks with her. But I can only see the wheelchair. God speaks to her although I can't understand a word she says.

As the words echoed in my mind, the Holy Spirit revealed just how much He loves and cares for us in such an individual and intimate way. She was not just another patient. She was someone special. Our commonality in Christ appeared as she faintly tapped her hand and nodded her head, trying to convey to me the love she had for her Lord. Here was the minister being ministered to by a little old saint.

She and the Holy Spirit taught me a new appreciation for the words and music we often sing so glibly. One day that little old lady from the nursing home and I will meet around the throne to sing praises to Jesus Christ together.

Lord, I pray that You'll never let me take the ministry of Your songs and the blessing of Your people for granted again.

Second, But Not Second Best

Here's to you, all the second players. Here's a salute, a tribute, recognition for all who labor faithfully and anonymously, playing second cornet, second horn, second trombone and second baritone. You are second part players, not with the connotation of flawed merchandise or factory rejects, but only in terms of the part played. You may be second, but you're never second best.

It seems like folks only remember the guys playing the flashy parts. Audiences come away dazzled by the E–flat soprano player who zooms through the musical stratosphere playing at the upper range of human hearing. They come away remembering the digital dexterity of the euphonium player as he prances chromatically up and down the staff.

They remember the thundering bombast of the trombone and tuba that sounds like a cross between New York's Eighth Avenue subway and an eruption of Mount St. Helens. They appreciate the solo cornets, with their ability to couple multiple tonguing with lightning speed on the valves. People also recall the sonorous, haunting tone of the E–flat horn as it emulates their French horn comrades.

But who ever comes away from a festival with comments such as, "Did you hear how precise those afterbeats were executed by the second horn player? What clarity! What technique!" Or perhaps, "Did you hear how clearly the second cornet honked out the melody two octaves below the rest of the band?"

It appears that for those who play second parts the only reward will be obscurity and possibly hyperventilation from all those afterbeats.

Second players do tend to feel a bit left out. After all, we remember the greats from all sports. But who ever remembers the backup NFL quarterback who has not played two minutes in his entire 12–year career? Or what about the backup third baseman with 15 career–at–bats? And who remembers the anonymous linemen of the NFL covered in mud, blood and trainer's tape who make it possible for the flashy running backs to scamper down the field to score?

Who remembers the unknown film actor? If he is in a western or a war movie, you can be sure that he'll be killed off long before they ever get to John Wayne.

The second player may be back there for a variety of reasons. He may be a new or relatively inexperienced player needing a place to break into the band. But in many cases, strong, reliable, musical craftsmen balance the total musical presentation of the band. Many could handle the solo and first parts, but most will serve faithfully as solid players who carry their parts with pride and dedication.

"The body is a unit, though it is made up of many parts; and though all its parts are many, they form one body. So it is with Christ" (1 Cor. 12:12). And so it is with a band.

Don't despair because you are unknown. You are contributing a very special part to the total performance of the body—of the band. Without you there would be glaring gaps in the music that would be as jarring as driving through a Manhattan pothole!

It might be nice if all the noted Salvation Army composers wrote special selections just for the second players, where the back benchers have a chance to shine. Might be fun. Second players—this one's for you! Go get 'em!

The Greatest Christmas Music Never Recorded

If you are like most people, after a blessed and busy Christmas season, you probably feel lucky to have survived with your sanity and your finances intact. With all the crowds, shopping, toys, parties, pageants and such, it is a wonder we make it through at all.

I think the music of Christmas makes the pace bearable, for it is at Christmas that we hear some of the finest music ever written. Unfortunately we have some of the worst too.

We have beautiful carols and songs such as the "Hallelujah Chorus," "Silent Night," "O Little Town," "O Holy Night" and others. We even have some more modern favorites such as "Do You Hear What I Hear?"

These sacred songs are contrasted with such well–known secular classics as "Silver Bells" and "White Christmas." I have a broad tolerance for almost any Christmas music, including Muzak arrangements suitable only for elevators and doctors' offices. But I do draw the line at "Jingle Bells" performed by barking dogs.

With regard to Salvation Army music, I have a loving respect for our little green carol book. This is high praise indeed coming from an exhausted cornet–playing corps officer who has gone through the book this past season what seems like 842 times. And the last 840 were played from memory.

Christmas music not only can raise the soul to new heights of adoration and praise, it can also contribute to the annual high of depression and suicide cases brought on by loneliness and despair. When you are alone and can't get home, "I'll Be Home for Christmas" can sometimes be too painful to bear.

The most beautiful Christmas music I have ever experienced was not performed in a church or in a concert hall but on a snow–covered mountain in north–central Pennsylvania. A few of the corps folks tried to broaden the education of this city boy and managed to get me out on the mountain at 5:00 am to get a crack at my first deer. As I trudged up the mountain with my rifle, boots, orange safety gear, license and ten layers of insulated clothing, I looked a bit like the cartoon of the Michelin tire man.

I never did get a huge, racked buck, but in the cold sunrise I was treated to a personal Christmas concert. The wild turkeys (out of season of course) gobbled their praises in the thick brush farther up the mountain. The chattering squirrels chimed in their song in the trees above me.

"Hark! The Herald Angels Sing" echoed in my mind's ear as the first rays of blissfully warming sunshine came over the ridge to the east. In the carol the angels made the announcement. In my case the angel was a very large red crested woodpecker who chirped his Morse code message of "good will to all men."

Below me several miles away the sounds of the rushing Schuylkill River cheered me with its merrily reverberating rendition of "Joy to the World" as it rushed on its way to Philadelphia.

I had hoped to see an eight point buck leading the way through the clearing ahead as one of "We Three Kings." But all I saw and heard were a few graceful and out of season does performing a woodland ballet like the "Nutcracker Suite."

My hunting partner farther up the mountain enjoyed his own Christmas concert. I do know for sure that when the hunt was over and he was able to warm his cold feet, it was definitely "As with Gladness."

To some people, a few hours hunting would be considered a foolish waste of time, especially for a busy corps officer. At best it would be lonely and boring. But in the silence and solitude, away from the phone and the pressure of the Christmas effort, and in the company of a few good friends and Christian brothers, it was a very valuable use of time for me.

In the deep forest carpeted with a lily white layer of snow, God had a chance to break in on my busy Christmas. He came to me not in church with a cornet in my hand but at the base of a tree at sunup. After all, you need to be absolutely still if you want to see a skittish deer, and in that setting you can truly "Be still, and know that [God is] God" (Ps. 46:10).

He announced His comforting and calming presence, reminding this harried officer of the good news of Jesus' birth. As the angel choir sang to the shepherds on that first Christmas long ago, God had the choir of the woods sing for me:

This is my Father's world
And to my listening ears;
All nature sings and round me rings
The music of the spheres.

This is my Father's world
The birds their carols raise;
The morning light, the lily white
Declare their Maker's praise.
                        (Maltbie Davenport Babcock)

If Handel had been with me in the woods that morning, together we would have jumped for joy and cheered "Hallelujah!" for the greatest concert ever heard by that small, yet very appreciative audience. For this message of calm assurance to a musician child of God, I gave the Lord a standing ovation.

We Have Nothing
to Fear

On March 4, 1933, President Franklin D. Roosevelt pronounced these great words in his first inaugural address: "The only thing we have to fear is fear itself." He was referring to the feeling of panic and utter despair experienced by a nation in the grip of a global economic depression.

Maybe President Roosevelt was an expert at running the country or even an expert on fear, but apparently he wasn't a musician, for whether you are a songster, timbrelist or instrumentalist, there are times when fear seems to take over. At those times you are no longer in charge; you are at the mercy of your trembling nerves.

Fear can manifest itself in shaking, sweating hands or wobbly, trembling knees that seem almost unable to support the weight of the terror–struck musician. This trembling is just slightly less violent than the shakes associated with a case of malaria or jungle fever.

Fear can erase months of preparation in seconds. It is as if someone left a magnet next to the practice tapes of your brain, erasing everything on it. I have seen vocalists panic and start in the wrong key and brass players who are usually a model of machine–like precision become absent–minded, fumble–fingered foulups.

All of us from time to time have suffered from one symptom of fear— "cotton mouth." This has nothing to do with rattlesnakes, but rather with the abrupt and total shutdown of the salivary glands that instantly turns the mouth into a mini–desert that makes playing, swallowing and even talking almost impossible.

What causes this fear anyway? Sometimes it can be caused by playing or singing in front of your peers or parents during a performance of the "Rock Bottom Band" at music camp or at a Congress or festival at the Royal Albert Hall.

As for me, I don't know the meaning of the word fear. But terror, horror, anxiety, trepidation, fright, panic—I know all of those!

At one festival, there was one very soft, high part that I was alone on. I was the only person playing in the house. I could almost feel and hear the beads of sweat fall and splash down the back of my neck. The words of

Psalm 22 came back to me only to increase my misery. "My God, my God, why have You forsaken me? Why are You so far from saving me? ... All who see me mock me; they hurl insults, shaking their heads ... My strength is dried up ... and my tongue sticks to the roof of my mouth; You lay me in the dust of death" (vs. 1,7,15). Amazing what the terror–filled mind can do.

"Lord, I don't ask for riches, glory or fame. Please help me not to mess up. Amen." Immediately my mind shifted to the Psalms again: "The Lord is my light and my salvation—whom shall I fear? The Lord is the stronghold of my life—of whom shall I be afraid?" (Ps. 27:1).

With the prayer, the fear passed. Was I nervous and excited? Yes, but not afraid. And as I claimed this promise to release the fear so I could play and praise God, I recall being calm and full of energy as I played my part perfectly at the top of my form.

President Roosevelt had the right idea after all. But I think David said it better: "Wait for the Lord; be strong and take heart" (Ps. 27:14).

Hey, we really do have nothing to fear—but fear itself.

The Thrill of Victory—
The Agony of Defeat

For years TV viewers have tuned in to see sports coverage on ABC's *Wide World of Sports*. You hear their famous quote at the beginning of the show, "the thrill of victory" as a team cheers their award–winning champion on a well– deserved win. Then you hear "the agony of defeat" as that poor, unfortunate ski jumper falls off the edge of the ramp, crashing in a heap. After watching him crash week after week, I wondered if he survived the fall. Fortunately, he is alive and well.

Yet, had he made the jump, he would have placed well out of medal winning range and been relegated to the anonymity he deserved. By being an apparent failure, he became famous. Sometimes in our musicianship, our failures and defeats can become some of our greatest victories.

Romans 8:28 really does work: "In all things God works for the good of those who love Him ..." It doesn't say that everything that happens to us will be good, but that all things will work out for our good. Sometimes, things just don't work out the way we planned. Yet sometimes a catastrophic defeat can lead to a shining victory.

A number of years ago I was playing on a band tour in Jamaica. During one of the festivals we were having a difficult time staying awake, since we had spent a good part of the day on the beach. We were plowing through Leslie Condon's "Call of the Righteous" when all of a sudden the bandmaster took the last section faster than ever. We were flying!

In reality, the bandmaster had a small lizard crawling up the inside of his pant leg. The more he shook and squirmed to remove the offending reptile, the faster he conducted. The faster he went, the faster we went. We never played the piece better, and at reunions the story gets bigger and better with each telling.

There are times when everything goes perfectly, from the national anthem to the postlude. And there are those times when everything comes crashing down around you. On those days you feel like that poor, battered ski jumper.

Another event I recall deals with feelings of defeat and victory. We were playing at youth councils and had murdered Morley Calvert's "Canadian

Folk Song Suite." We were terrible. In fact we had to stop and restart three times! We were humiliated in front of our peers, ruining the music and our reputations.

I think we needed that defeat to fully appreciate times of victory. The Lord taught us that any victory won was His and not ours. "The eyes of the arrogant man will be humbled and the pride of men brought low; the Lord alone will be exalted in that day" (Isa. 2:11). We were humbled and then some.

Later that weekend we played another Calvert piece, "For Our Transgressions." We played the piece with uncommon sensitivity. Without other prodding than that of the Holy Spirit, one by one we put down our instruments and made our way to the altar to rededicate our lives to Jesus Christ.

What had been a humiliation and a defeat was now a glorious victory, not just because we played the music correctly, but because Jesus took us and changed us by that experience. We couldn't have fully appreciated the thrill of God's victory without experiencing the agony of defeat. I'm glad we experienced both.

Indiana Jones and the Bandroom of Doom

"If adventure has a name—it's Indiana Jones." That is how the studio promoted Steven Spielberg's film *Indiana Jones and the Temple of Doom*. Spielberg has given us some great action movies in the Indiana Jones trilogy. Hey, I still get shivers when Jones goes into the Indian temple ruins and nearly gets flattened by a runaway boulder.

Fearless Dr. Jones, professor of archaeology, is prepared to risk life and limb anywhere on the globe to search for some archaeological treasure. Arrayed in his now famous fedora, leather jacket and bull whip, he will tackle any adversary in his quest for fortune and glory.

At times I have felt like Indiana Jones. I have never searched for the Ark of the Covenant or any other ancient treasure, but I have dared to search for a particular piece of music in the Bandroom of Doom.

I can almost hear the stirring theme of the John Williams soundtrack as I don my fedora and leather jacket to face unknown dangers. With great stealth and care, I pass by the twin sentinels guarding the entrance to the band room—two enormous, gray, rotting shells of what used to be a couple of B–flat basses. They seem to warn me to turn back and abandon this foolhardy adventure before I get hurt.

I gingerly tiptoe past the "Twins," avoiding the poisonous touch of their encrusted tarnish. No sooner have I cleared them than I enter the minefield. The minefield is not filled with explosives but rather with junk—instrument cases of all types and sizes, boxes of *War Crys* left over from 1974, Christmas supplies and drum equipment. All of this is crammed into a very confined space, waiting in ambush to grab me by the ankle as I step over them. At worst I may fall, sustaining a serious injury. At best I'll ruin a good pair of uniform pants in the ordeal.

Slithering down from the walls and shelves come the uncoiling snakes of old speaker wire, microphone cables and extension cords. If the minefield doesn't get me, the snakes might.

Finally, after much care and labor I pass by all of the obstacles and reach the inner cabinet in the Bandroom of Doom. Here I begin my search for the elusive second cornet book.

I hear my heart pounding as I ease the drawer open, fearing that some demented band librarian has left a booby–trapped *Unity Series* score to pounce upon some unsuspecting trespasser. Luckily for me there are no traps—only a big mess.

The cavernous drawer holds the entire corps' music library. There are ripped and faded Christmas carol books. There are old *Gems for Songsters* scattered amid *Salvation Army Song Books*, all held together with liberal applications of red cloth tape. Random parts and scores of many different series of music mix with a wild assortment of sheet music, old programs and mismatched drum sticks. In the back of the drawer I find a small treasure box filled with antique gems—old valves and caps, lyres, lyre screws, mouthpieces and spit valve corks.

Strangely enough, there is an entire section of music still hermetically sealed in the original plastic packing. It is a perfectly complete band score to *The Holy War.*

Alternately wheezing and sneezing from the mildew and dust, I carefully pick through the rubble and locate the second cornet book I was searching for. But just as I breathe a sigh of relief that my quest is finally ended, I bump a hidden switch. Now as if things weren't bad enough, the walls are closing in on me! The place was claustrophobic before, but now the room may squash me as it has other musicians foolish enough to challenge its hidden mysteries.

Indiana Jones hates snakes. I hate music stands. They never fold up and pack neatly. The walls converge as music stands prepare to impale me on their spindly, metal legs.

Hurdling as fast as I can, I leap past the stands, duck under the cable snakes and, catching my trusty bull whip on an overhanging pipe, manage to swing over the minefield. Desperate and exhausted I face the Twins. I am too tired to run, so I pull out my trusty .44 and shoot them.

I call upon my last ounce of energy and stagger out of the Bandroom of Doom into the corps hall. I made it back alive with my second cornet music!

So what if I have a hole in my uniform pants and I'm covered with spider webs, cuts and bruises? I have won. I have finished the course and have emerged victorious.

"Sorry to trouble you, Cap', but we goofed. We needed the second horn, not the second cornet. Could you go back into the bandroom to get it, please?"

The Right Stuff

Tom Wolfe's book *The Right Stuff* honored the bravery and quiet courage of our first American astronauts. It focused on the men of the Mercury space program who were the first Americans in space. Much of the book is devoted to those who pushed the limits of aviation technology far beyond the sound barrier. Not since the days of World War II had such a total commitment of mind, imagination and will been made to such a task—the exploration of space.

At first we were awed by the power and majesty of space exploration. Later we became rather ho–hum about it. We watched the space shuttle blast off and return to Earth with all the excitement of watching the crosstown bus until the day Challenger exploded in a ball of fire just 73 seconds into its mission, killing all seven crew members aboard.

We had watched rockets go up so smoothly and effortlessly that we had forgotten how dangerous space travel really is. Crew members were well aware of the dangers involved. They knew that they might be killed or marooned in space with little or no hope of rescue. Still they were willing to risk those dangers to increase our knowledge. They had the courage to let their deeds, rather than their words, speak for them. They had "the right stuff."

Those astronauts were dedicated to going higher, faster, farther than ever before. They never paraded their accomplishments and never spoke of their fears. They chose to let their courage show in their actions.

How many Salvationist musicians have the right stuff? Every band or songster group knows someone who just gets by in rehearsal and performance, puting forth no more effort than is absolutely necessary.

Musically speaking, we are living in exciting times. The music written by modern Salvationist composers is more technically demanding than ever before. No longer do second players play only afterbeats. From the most gifted to the least capable, we must with courage and determination put forth the effort required to excel.

You have probably met people who have told you how good they were once upon a time. But the Lord requires us to be doers, not talkers. Push the envelope of your skills to the limit and beyond. It requires a commit-ment of time and talent. But only when you have faced your fears and done your best to master the music will it honor God.

Bandsman Joshua had the right stuff. He had to play a difficult festival in a hostile country outside the fortified walls of Jericho. He didn't have to come through the earth's atmosphere with a defective heat shield like John Glenn. Neither did he have to pilot a crippled craft without navigational instruments like Gordon Cooper. Still, he risked personal danger as he test-ed his faith in God.

At that festival, Joshua proved that he was God's man. He displayed loy-alty, bravery and an unshakable faith in God, in spite of the dangers involved. Joshua let his actions speak for his faith in the Lord. Can we do any less?

I Love It When a Plan Comes Together

One of my favorite TV shows featured a group of four soldiers of fortune who fought for the rights of the oppressed and downtrodden. They made all manner of homemade weapons and wrecked almost as many cars as General Motors makes, firing thousands of rounds from their automatic weapons while never injuring anyone. They were the A–Team.

The leader of the A–Team, Hannibal Smith, utters a favorite phase when all of their plans go awry and they are captured, beaten, tortured and hopelessly outnumbered. Out of this chaos he grins and says, "I love it when a plan comes together."

In his career Hannibal Smith must have travelled with a Salvation Army music group, for it seems every trip with every group is filled with broken plans and frayed nerves. It might be a world tour or just a day trip, but in terms of the planning and frustration, it's a major event.

Just about the time you are set to load the bus, at least one kid arrives late. The leader makes sure that everyone has the necessary equipment—instruments, uniforms, hats/caps, music, etc., so nothing will go wrong. Imagine his frustration as he hears two percussionists arguing at the airport terminal, "I thought you packed the bass drum!" "No. *You* said you were going to pack it." Imagine the sinking feeling when they realize that neither of them packed the bass drum.

Once while travelling with a band we lost a complete case of music. We found it eventually, though we had to revise that evening's festival to work around the missing parts. Not a very good beginning to a five–day concert tour.

I'm a firm believer in Murphy's Law, which states that "If anything can go wrong, it will." Its corollary further states, "The thing that will go wrong is the thing that will hurt you the most." How true!

A recurring nightmare of mine always comes the night before a big festival. I'm all set to play but I can't find my mouthpiece. Someone, trying to be funny, has hidden it. In my dream I search all over for it and try to borrow one. Unfortunately the only guys who have an extra mouthpiece are tuba players.

It could be worse. We could have boarded the wrong plane or had our equipment end up somewhere else. Not too long ago a young man boarded a plane he thought was going to Oakland, California only to discover after an unusually long flight that it was bound for Auckland, New Zealand

Perhaps in all of these mishaps Satan wants us to be so angry and upset that we can't fully appreciate the music we play and sing. But along the way, the faithful practice and preparation pays off; it all works out fine. People are blessed. And you give thanks to God who makes order from the chaos of plans gone haywire. You say with calm assurance, "I love it when a plan comes together."

Paul, a member of the original A–Team (A for apostle), said it a bit differently. "We know that in all things God works for the good of those who love Him, who have been called according to His purpose" (Rom. 8:28 KJV). I think even Hannibal Smith would have to agree.

Once Upon
a Kettle

Over the years people have come to expect Army music at Christmastime. "It just isn't Christmas without The Salvation Army," they say. For Salvationists, Christmas just wouldn't be Christmas without the annual kettle appeal. Hundreds of players, singers and bell ringers can be seen in action next to the familiar red "Sharing is Caring" sign at kettles on street corners and shopping malls across the country. I'd like to salute those who give of their time, skill and energy during this blessed and hectic season.

Since I'm from the Northeast, most of my kettle experience has involved December cold. On those days when the valves on my cornet are frozen and my feet are numb, I envy those fortunate souls in Florida and Southern California who play Christmas carols in shirt sleeves, while I am clothed in enough layers to make me nearly bulletproof.

But how can they fully appreciate "Dashing through the snow in a one horse open sleigh" in the shade of a palm tree?

However, painful, cold and lonely standing kettles is, no other time of year makes people more receptive to the gospel message. Hard hearts are made soft. Often this comes as a result of the quiet majesty and power of the carols we play, such as "O Come All Ye Faithful." Even the most cynical soul is blessed by the innocent smile of a newborn baby—especially when the baby is the Christ child.

Playing for kettles isn't easy. There you stand song after song, hour after hour, trying not to quit or freeze. It seems most difficult when you play or sing all alone with people watching you as if you are from another planet. Still, most bandsmen or songsters I know would rather play or sing for six hours than ring a bell for one.

I must admit that I hate having to chase my uniform cap down the street in a 50 mph gale–force wind. I hate being mistaken for the doorman at the Sheraton because of the S on my uniform! But I like Christmas kettles! I love the Lord and the love He expressed by giving His Son Jesus to be our Savior. I like to watch the people who need to hear that good news of the Savior. I love to join in the celebration and proclamation of the Savior's birth. In fact, I feel a bit like one of the angelic heralds announcing the good news of Jesus for all to hear:

> *Hark! The herald angels sing:*
> *Glory to the newborn King;*
> *Peace on earth, and mercy mild,*
> *God and sinners reconciled.*
> *Joyful, all ye nations rise,*
> *Join the triumph of the skies;*
> *With the angelic host proclaim,*
> *Christ is born in Bethlehem.*
> *Hark! The herald angels sing;*
> *Glory to the newborn King.*
>
> (Charles Wesley)

You Look Mahhhvelous!

In a spoof of the super–macho male type Billy Crystal used to parody the speech and mannerisms of the late Fernando Lamas. Crystal's Hernando tells us in his broadly affected Latin accent, "Dahlings. You looook mahhhvelous. And you know it is better to look mahhhvelous than to be mahhhvelous. And dahling you look mahhhvelous."

His spoof causes us to look more honestly at ourselves than we might care to. We in The Salvation Army take great pride in looking marvelous with our uniforms and our gleaming brass instruments. We love to see our flag of yellow, red and blue waving boldly in the breeze. But when we get behind the uniforms and the instruments and the music, maybe we place too much importance on looking marvelous rather than actually being marvelous. I refer not to how we look and perform but to how we have allowed God to work in us and through us as Christians.

A simple pleasure that I have come to enjoy is hunting wild turkey. A few hours in God's woods with a few close Christian brothers is time well spent. The clever and elusive wild turkey possesses acute vision and hearing, unlike the domesticated turkey on your table this Thanksgiving. For wily old Tom, I must go into the woods dressed in full camouflage so that when I'm hunkered down by a big tree, I'm almost invisible.

But that old bird knows that the clump of mottled green, brown and black doesn't belong in his forest. He knows that the hen call I'm using isn't a desirable lady turkey. I even think he knows the range of my shotgun and stops just beyond it to strut and dance and drive me crazy. I look marvelous—to me at least. But somehow that turkey can see right through me, camouflage and all.

As a bandsman, I was expert at camouflage as well. Maybe you are, too. One can look like a "good Salvationist" without making a full commitment to Jesus Christ. It wasn't until I made that commitment of heart, mind and will that in God's grace I could feel marvelous. To Jesus I am marvelous even if no one else recognizes it. The Lord saw that I was hiding from Him behind my well–tailored uniform and shiny cornet. I hadn't fooled anyone but myself.

Once I heard a very ordinary–looking saint of God sing "Amazing Grace." She did not look marvelous in her uniform, and she certainly didn't sound marvelous. She changed keys every third note! But she sang with such conviction and joy that it would have put the "beautiful people" to shame. She won't ever be asked to sing at the Royal Albert Hall, but she will sing her praises before the throne of God. After all, she has been down here practicing for it.

It's fine to look good. It's our Christian duty to be the very best we can be so that our music and our lives bring glory to God. But don't just *look* marvelous—*be* marvelous.

III.

———— ◆ ————

Radical Wit & Wisdom

If King Solomon was really the wisest man of all time, why did he have 300 wives and countless numbers of live–in girlfriends? That doesn't sound too smart to me. Every day after work it was, "Hi, Honey! I'm home ... Hi, Honey! I'm home ... Hi, Honey! I'm home ..."—300 times! By the time he was done greeting all of his wives and girlfriends, it was time to go back to work. Don't even think about remembering birthdays and anniversaries!

But Solomon did give some good advice, even if he didn't always follow it himself: "My son, pay attention to what I say; listen closely to my words. Do not let them out of your sight, keep them within your heart; for they are life to those who find them and health to a man's whole body. Above all else, guard your heart, for it is the wellspring of life" (Prov. 4:20–23).

Hey, learning and living is not a spectator sport, although you can learn much from observing life as it happens all around you every day. If you ask the Lord, He will show you all manner of fun things along your journey. The Lord promises: "Call to Me and I will answer you and tell you great and unsearchable things you do not know" (Jer. 33:3).

Lord, help me to keep my eyes open and see Your great things going on all around me—and to be amazed!

No Artificial Anything

A trip through the grocery store to find food that is nutritious, wholesome and all–natural can be frustrating. It seems as if nothing these days contains the genuine ingredients of past generations. I know that we live in a technologically advanced society that places a premium on shelf life and dietary benefit, but there are few things that can compare to your grandmother's homemade bread and pies for sheer eating pleasure. And best of all, those goodies contain no artificial anything.

Most of the food these days has something added to ensure uniformity of taste, consistency and freshness. As a result, reading the ingredients on food packages becomes more an exercise in chemistry than in the culinary arts.

In the days before refrigeration, meats were salted or turned into jerky to keep them from going rancid. Jerky is quite tasty, though it may seem you're gnawing on a baseball glove when you sit down to Sunday dinner. Now there is Alar to keep apples red for months and sodium nitrates to keep hot dogs and lunch meats fresh for weeks rather than days.

As with the ancient Egyptians, archaeologists may discover our mummified remains at a dig site 10,000 years from now—without our having to resort to embalming. All we need are sufficiently ingested amounts of polysorbate 90 "to retard spoilage."

Many of the foods we eat can hardly be considered food at all. At one corps appointment we received a donation of "apple drink." Upon closer examination, we noted that the manufacturer was careful to add the disclaimer "contains no juice." Perhaps the closest this stuff ever got to an apple was in driving past an orchard in a tanker truck on the way to and from the laboratory.

Here are some modern ingredients that should bring better eating through chemistry:

Ingredients: enriched flour (wheat), niacin, reduced iron, thiamine mononitrate, riboflavin, corn syrup, vegetable shortening (partially hydrogenated soybean and/or palm oil with or without mono and diglycerides), sugar, cocoa drops (with decithin and vanillin), whey, oats and/or barley, wheat nuts, molasses, salt, sodium bicarbonate, ammonium bicarbonate, artificial flavorings, lecithin, modified food starch, sorbic acid (preservative).

Translation: chocolate chip cookie

Technically, it may be a cookie, but not like mom used to make, unless mom happens to be a research chemist! There's nothing like the taste of fresh, homemade food from scratch rather than from a freeze–dried, microwavable packet, filled with all manner of polysyllabic chemicals.

Scripture tells of an interesting occasion when the Lord provided food that was fresh each day and could not be stored for the next day—even using Tupperware! When the Hebrew slaves left Egypt for the promised land of Canaan, they complained that there was nothing to eat. There were no fast food eateries anywhere along the way. If they didn't bring it or grow it, there was no food. The Lord in His divine kindness provided heavenly food out in the desert—*manna*:

"In the morning there was a layer of dew around the camp. When the dew was gone, thin flakes like frost on the ground appeared on the desert floor. When the Israelites saw it, they said to each other, 'What is it?' For they did not know what it was. Moses said to them 'It is the bread the Lord has given you to eat'" (Exod. 16:13–15).

The word *manna* means "What is it?" I must have eaten *manna* on many occasions at camp or at school without knowing it, because we were never sure of the origin of some of our food. It may have come from an animal, but we weren't always sure of the species.

Manna had to be used on the day of delivery, making it useless for left-overs. Some folks tried to stash a little away so they wouldn't have to make the daily *manna* run, only to discover that overnight it rotted and was unfit to eat.

Granted there was not much variation in the menu, and I am sure every Israelite family had to learn a thousand recipes for preparing *manna* in ways that were new and appealing. But it was fresh, and it was free, and it kept them alive.

God sent *manna* fresh each day the way He sends His grace and love. He never holds back, for grace, like eating, is an ongoing process. Like clockwork, my stomach knows when it's mealtime; it makes its demands known by its familiar growl. I can't eat only once and never again just as I can't partake of the grace of God once and no more.

Grace is fresh, free, without artificial motive, artificial kindness, artificial caring or artificial love. It is fresh each day, yet based in things eternal. It needs no refrigeration, for the preservative is the unchanging nature of God.

"So let your conversation be always full of grace, seasoned with salt [with no artificial flavors, colors or preservatives with just enough zip to have a little tang in the taste] so that you will be able to answer everyone" (Col. 4:16). And do it with true and honest Christian love.

It would be terrible if people looked to us for a practical application of Jesus' love and grace at work in our lives and saw instead the disclaimer "contains no Christ." We need to be filled with the grace and goodness of God, with no artificial anything.

Today Is a Good Day to Die

It was hot Sunday afternoon on June 25, 1876 on a remote stretch of prairie along the Little Big Horn River in the Montana Territory. Chief Sitting Bull, medicine man and chief of the Hunkpapa Sioux, was preparing his people to move down the valley in search of buffalo and grass for their ponies. The last thing he expected was the charge of the 7th U.S. Cavalry in what has come to be called "Custer's Last Stand."

On the day of the battle, Lt. Colonel George Custer split his command, sending Captain Frederick Benteen on a reconnaissance mission while Major Marcus Reno moved headlong down the Little Big Horn valley. His charge placed him at maximum risk since he attacked the strongest portion of the Hunkpapa camp. At the same time, Custer counterattacked at what he thought was the end of the Indian encampment. Unfortunately, he entered the middle of the Cheyenne and Oglala Sioux villages with disastrous consequences. Custer, his brothers Tom and Boston, his nephew and namesake Armstrong Reed and his brother–in–law Tom Calhoun were killed at the Battle of the Little Big Horn along with the officers, enlisted men and scouts of his detachment.

According to Sioux and Cheyenne accounts, Chief Sitting Bull rallied his warriors by reminding them to "take courage. Today is a good day to die." As was their practice, the warriors wrote their death songs long before the battle. In this case, the songs were current since Sitting Bull and the others had just defeated a regiment of infantry and calvary under the command of Brig. General George Crook at the Battle of the Rosebud on June 17.

The songs recounted their adventures, accomplishments and aspirations for their posterity in anticipation of the day when they would fall in battle. Having prepared their eulogies in advance, they counted themselves as already dead. If the final blow came, they were ready since it was "a good day to die"—with no regrets over loose ends or unfinished business.

The Apostle Paul was not a Sioux warrior, but he too recorded his death song:

"For I am already being poured out like a drink offering, and the time has come for my departure. I have fought the good fight, I have finished the race, I have kept the faith. Now there is in store for me the crown of righteousness, which the Lord, the righteous Judge, will award to me on that day—and not only to me, but also to all who have longed for His appearing" (2 Tim. 4:6–8).

Paul prepared to leave this world and his ministry with no sadness over things left unsaid or undone. An expert in Scripture from his Pharisee days, he probably remembered the words of Psalm 118:24: "This is the day the Lord has made; let us rejoice and be glad in it."

Some days it seems as if we will never achieve the level of calm and success we deserve. We may feel that once we accept Jesus as Savior and Lord we will never have a problem again. And if we do have problems, we suspect that our Christian commitment is flawed.

The Lord taught us to pray, "give us this day our daily bread ..." Problems, pain, crises and disasters make up our daily bread as surely as freedom, serenity and peace. We need to work through all portions of our daily bread with rejoicing, accepting the challenge to grow in Christ, remembering that nothing can separate us from the love of Jesus Christ our Lord. We can overcome every crisis experience—nakedness, danger, war, famine, hardship, persecution, angels or demons, things present, things past or future or even death itself (Rom. 8:35–39).

Paul's death song includes a note of preparation for his future martyrdom, knowing that his life and future were safe with Jesus Christ. "None of us lives to himself alone and none of us dies to himself alone," he said. "If we live, we live to the Lord; and if we die, we die to the Lord. So, whether we live or die, we belong to the Lord" (Rom. 14:7–8). He felt confident that whether he lived to enjoy long years or was killed for the sake of the message of Christ at an early age, it was worth it all. Paul was as dedicated to the cause of Christ as Crazy Horse and the others were to protecting their homeland from the U.S. Cavalry. Death was not to be desired or sought after, but it was not to be feared either: "To live is Christ and to die is gain" (Phil. 1:21).

In fact, Paul was torn between his desire to minister—to preach salvation, build churches and disciple new pastors—and his desire to see Jesus face to face. He knew that his life in this tangible, physical world was a gift from Jesus Christ. It was not to be hoarded or conserved, but spent in the Lord's service. Paul counted himself already dead as far as sin and the old nature of rebellion was concerned. "I have been crucified with Christ," he declared, "and I no longer live, but Christ lives in me" (Gal. 2:20). The old sinful pattern of life was dead, and it mattered little to the Apostle when and how the physical body caught up to his eternal spirit.

Commanded to be brave soldiers of Jesus, we put on the full armor of God and write our death song which is really a song of eternal life through Jesus Christ. Other accomplishments will be forgotten—only the things of God will last forever. We can take courage, for today is a better day to live.

Live Long
and Prosper

It hardly seems possible that it has been 25 years since we first heard of the voyages of the Starship Enterprise with its mission "to explore new worlds, to seek out new life and to boldly go where no man has gone before." This television creation from the fertile imagination of Gene Roddenberry has been a regular guest in our homes, even though it only ran for three years on network television before it was canceled due to poor ratings. But after years of successful syndication, six feature films and several new generations of series, this adventure classic has indeed had a very long and profitable life. Pieces of the set and the miniature starship are on display at The National Air and Space Museum in Washington, D.C.

Once decried as nothing more than "Wagon Train to the stars," "Star Trek" has provided a full career for several actors and actresses whose characters have nearly taken on lives of their own. Most people who watch U.S. television are familiar with the names of Captain James T. Kirk, Chief Engineer Scott, Dr. "Bones" McCoy, Sulu, Chekov and Uhura. And almost everyone knows the famed, pointy–eared, logically minded science officer, Mr. Spock.

Spock is best known for his dispassionate, completely logical approach to life, his ability to keep his head while all those about him were losing theirs. While Captain Kirk contemplated the meaning of a galaxy filled with beautiful women and Bones complained about Spock's lack of emotion, Spock went efficiently about his work saving the universe from Romulans, Tribbles and assorted Klingons. Even when Engineer Scott whined about each new episodic crisis, Spock remained unflustered. When Scotty reported that the warp drive could only operate in reverse, the dilithium crystals were burned and there was no Cherry Coke in the commissary, it didn't phase the unflappable Spock.

"Aye Captain," Scotty would complain, "we can't hold orbit much longer. We'll burn up in the planet's atmosphere in eight minutes." To this Spock would reply, "We'll all die in 7.88714309 minutes. Let's try to be precise, Mr. Scott."

Perhaps the most lasting legacy that Mr. Spock and "Star Trek" has given us is the Vulcan splay–fingered greeting of "live long and prosper." That greeting accurately sums up our obsession with longevity of life and financial prosperity. The "good life" means abundant duration with all the trappings of affluence and financial success that go with it.

We are a nation of fitness freaks who spend fortunes to look and feel healthy. We join health clubs, invest in the latest exercise equipment, endure tummy tucks, face lifts, liposuction, collagen injections, mega–dose vitamin regimens and bizarre diets, all in an attempt to look fit and live longer. Yet at the same time we eat more fat than any other nation on earth. We have children who are unfit because they don't participate in sports any more strenuous than Nintendo. We lead the world in heart disease, cancer and diabetes, while we spend billions of dollars every year on alcohol and drugs. The rate of HIV infection and AIDS is on the rise. We know that safe sex is assured not by use of condoms but by following the counsel of the Bible that stresses sexual abstinence before marriage and fidelity throughout the relationship. But we are usually unwilling or unable to break the pull of our destructive behaviors.

In addition to long life, we demand and expect economic prosperity. We want to own anything our hearts desire without having to endure unbearably long periods of savings or sacrifice. Perhaps that is why we Americans have such a self–destructive love affair with credit cards which make it possible to have the object of our desire immediately. Unfortunately we also have the resulting personal debt that may last longer than the items we purchased.

The Lord has some advice concerning the desire to "live long and prosper." He promises to the nation Israel and to us that if we follow the instruction of the Lord, we will reap tremendous benefit.

God often makes His promises conditional on our participation and obedience. That is not to say that grace is based on our performance, but it does mean that we have a part to play in our spiritual growth.

Jesus never healed or cleansed a person without receiving some degree of cooperation on their part. In the case of the man who was born crippled, Jesus told him that if he wanted to walk he had to pick up his mat and go. The act of forgiveness and healing required that he step out in faith and move toward the goal of health and well–being. Jesus never "zapped" anyone into health, forgiveness or prosperity without a challenge to faith and obedience.

Long life and prosperity have a basis in Scripture as well. Just before the children of Israel crossed into Canaan to inherit the promised land, culminating a 400–plus year journey from slavery to freedom, Moses shared God's message for their future. "Honor your father and your mother," he reminded them, "so that you may live long in the land the Lord your God is giving you" (Exod. 20:12). Good advice for children who may one day be parents with children and all the accompanying heartaches. He also advised the people to "keep His decrees and commands ... that you may live long in the land the Lord God gives you for all time" (Deut. 4:40). Moses added, "[These] are not just idle words for you—they are your life. By them you will live long in the land you are crossing the Jordan to possess" (Deut. 32:47).

Long life and prosperity are founded on what we do with our lives in obedience to the plan and program of God. They are not based on what we own, what we do, what we think we deserve, or what we have accomplished. In fact, quality of life is based on our relationship with Jesus Christ and what we do with what He has given in the amount of time allotted to us.

So in the best neo–Vulcan that I can muster, my prayer is for all of us to "walk in all the way that the Lord your God has commanded you, so that you may live and prosper and prolong your days" (Deut. 5:33).

G.O.D.—Guaranteed Overnight Delivery

While on my way to work, I was amazed to see God's truck coming down the highway. I knew it was God's truck since it had His name on it in big red letters—G.O.D. I knew He was omnipotent and omnipresent, but I had no idea He was a member of the Teamsters.

It was only after the truck got closer that I realized it was not God, "the Creator, Preserver, and Governor of all things" like the Salvation Army doctrine says, but a trucking company that promises "Guaranteed Overnight Delivery."

I must admit that I was a bit disappointed at first but ultimately encouraged by the fact that God does not promise "guaranteed overnight delivery" on all our wants, wishes and requests. He answers them in His way, in His time and according to His plan for our lives. He does promise that "If you believe, you will receive whatever you ask for in prayer" (Matt. 21:22), but it will be in the context of His will, His time and His way. God makes no assurances as to guaranteed overnight delivery, although there are times He moves at a much faster speed.

Sometimes we are told to "wait upon the Lord" (Isa. 40:31 KJV). In a society that demands instant gratification of every urge, whim and desire, we are notoriously poor at waiting for anything, including the Lord. We are obsessed with securing information in an instant. After all, we know what we want and we want it now. We have cellular phones in our cars and in our briefcases to keep us in constant communication. We have fax machines in our offices to secure instant data transmission even if it is only to make a lunch order at the local restaurant that caters to the business crowd. We have modems installed in our computers so we can exchange data (and games) between computers. We have become so accustomed to having what we want, when we want it that we have become extremely impatient when we have to wait a second or two to access information on the computer or to make our dinner in the microwave oven.

A century ago the Pony Express was able to deliver a letter in weeks rather than months. Compared to the regular mail service, the news was still fairly fresh except when people received a letter advising that a favorite relative was taken ill. They may have been dead and buried long before the relatives ever got the word. And as much as we complain about the Postal Service, it still gets mail delivered efficiently and—in most cases—on time. The Battle of New Orleans during the War of 1812 was fought weeks after the peace treaty was signed in Paris. Not good news for the casualties who didn't know the war was already over. But no one knew that. Now we can see the news half a world away at the instant it is happening. So it seems inevitable that we tend to become impatient when God takes longer to answer our prayers than we want Him to.

One of my favorite stories in Scripture concerning prayer is found in Acts 12:1–19. In this account, Peter is arrested and imprisoned by King Herod's men. The plan was to put Peter on public trial during Passover as a warning to discourage the spread of Christianity. While Peter was in jail, the church prayed for his safety and release. "So Peter was kept in prison, but the church was earnestly praying to God for him" (Acts 12:5).

While the people from the church were praying for Peter, an angel came and miraculously led him out of the jail completely undetected. Doors opened, chains fell off and guards slept soundly, allowing them to make their escape. But here is where it gets funny. Peter came to the house where the people were praying for him and knocked on the door. Not wishing to disturb the seriousness of their intercessory prayer, the elders sent a young girl named Rhoda to see who was making the commotion. Maybe they thought it was a salesman. When she came to the door, she was so excited to hear Peter's voice she forgot to open the door and let him inside! She ran back to tell the others, and we can just imagine the scene: "Hey everyone. Peter is outside!"

"Rhoda. Get a grip on yourself. We are doing serious prayer business here, and we don't have time for your foolishness."

"But I mean it. Peter really is here. He is outside."

"For the last time, girl. We have neither the patience nor the energy to put up with your crazy talk. We have things we have to pray about." And with that, they went back to their prayers. "Dear Lord, we most earnestly entreat You to look with kindness upon Your servant Peter who even as we speak is incarcerated in the jail of that intolerable King Herod ..."

Meanwhile Peter is still outside banging on the door eagerly hoping someone with some sense lets him in before he is arrested for disturbing the peace. And God is saying to them, "Get on with it. I already took care of that one!" "But Peter kept knocking, and when they opened the door and saw him, they were astonished" (12:16).

Why should we pray as if God has no intention of hearing let alone answering our prayers? Why should we go through the exercise of prayer and then act surprised when God answers it so quickly and decisively?

Some prayers He answers with a definite "no" regardless of how long we pray. Those prayers are either not according to His will or are not good for us or others. To some He says, "Keep on praying. The time is not right yet—or you are not right yet." But there are times when the Lord answers faster than we could have imagined. "Before they call I will answer; while they are still speaking I will hear" (Isa. 65:24). That makes "Guaranteed Overnight Delivery" seem like an eternity!

Your Permanent Record

"Young man, if you continue to misbehave, it will go on your permanent record." I am sure all of us have heard that dire warning from our teachers. Looking back, it was a "management by guilt" maneuver to get us to behave and to study. The emphasis was always on the words "permanent record," suggesting that every teacher, employer, credit manager, financial advisor and potential spouse would have perpetual free access to the unabridged dossier of our lives, that the information would follow us to the grave—and beyond.

The dreaded record is even more comprehensive than the one kept by Santa Claus. He knows only when we've been bad or good, but the permanent record catalogues each and every infraction of the rules. It lists each time you forgot your lunch money, the times you were late to class or forgot your homework (even if the dog *did* eat it) or you spoke without first raising your hand. It inventories your grades, deportment, effort, work habits, attendance and absences. The record hardly seems fair, for while it meticulously details each time you were late or absent, it fails to give adequate recognition for those times you went to school when you were legitimately ill just so you could keep your record of perfect attendance intact.

Some parents let their kids stay home for each sniffle or skinned knee. My mom was extremely difficult to convince of any medical emergency worthy of missing school. If I wasn't feeling well, all I needed to stay home from school was a note from the doctor—as long as the doctor was the county coroner.

Never does the permanent record show projects you took for the challenge rather than for the extra credit, or the books you read even though you did not have to do a book report on them. Never does it reflect the hours of work you and your parents invested in homework assignments and special projects.

No, the permanent record shows the time you got caught doing a perfect impression of Mr. Flingle, the school principal. Yet even he agreed that you did capture the essence of his public address announcements and showed real promise for a career in stand–up comedy.

But realistically—how permanent is permanent? Ten years, twenty years, thousands of years? Does every school keep the records of every student until 10 years after they graduate—or until their great–great grandchildren graduate? With my luck, they will still have a file on me until Mount Rushmore crumbles into gravel.

When I went to work as a civilian employee of the United States government, I was astonished to discover that they researched my school history and references all the way back to elementary school. I guess they wanted to know if I had any subversive leanings expressed or hostile threats in the second grade. Now the government has a full educational and work history complete with fingerprints.

The Salvation Army keeps a personnel file on me, and every other officer, that houses all the records of education, appointment, and service reviews until I am Promoted to Glory.

And all of us carry around a permanent record of our own as we keep careful mental lists of those individuals who have been kind or mean to us, those who have nurtured or affirmed us, or those who have betrayed or hurt us. We also keep a secret, detailed account of failures, fears, angers, broken promises and shattered dreams that we hope no one will ever see. It records criticism and cutting comments that are replayed over and over again in our minds. Some of the cruelest entries are those promises we made to God—to read our Bibles more often, to pray more, to witness more, to serve more, to live better for Him—but just couldn't do. We are like Paul who knew what he wanted to do but always ended up doing the very thing he did not want to do: "I have the desire to do what is good, but I cannot carry it out. For what I do is not the good I want to do; no, the evil I do not want to do—this I keep on doing" (Rom. 7:18–19), and it ends up indelibly printed in our permanent record.

Our minds catalogue all the times we were rejected or disappointed. We record all of the words that have caused anguish more intense and more scarring than physical blows. Sticks and stones may break my bones, but words harm with more lasting impact.

But even though our brains make permanent records of our memories, good and bad, there is good news. When Jesus Christ forgives us from sin and the penalty of sin with its haunting guilt and fear of death, He records our name in the Lamb's Book of Life. That permanent record of the redeemed is kept in the Lord's archives for all eternity where Satan cannot ever use the inventory of our sin to raise his accusations against us again.

When we are forgiven, Scripture states that the Lord takes the sin and the record of it and "as far as the east is from the west, so far has He removed our transgressions from us" (Ps.103:12).

When we are forgiven, God not only removes the listing of sin by our name but tears out the page, so it will never be held against us again. There is no Hall of Shame where the artifacts of our disobedience are kept on display or file copies of our sins kept for historical research. The record is removed and forgotten forever.

Perhaps the removal of his permanent record is why Paul wrote so enthusiastically about salvation and restoration. Paul knew how he actively persecuted the Church and took great delight in arresting and torturing Christians, all the while believing he was doing the Lord a favor. But once he was forgiven, he knew that God in His love keeps a different set of books. Paul noted in 1 Corinthians 13:5 that the love of Jesus Christ, the love that we are to accept and to share with others, "is not rude, it is not self-seeking, it is not easily angered, it keeps no record of wrongs."

That is good advice for us. Keep short accounts—do not catalogue all of the slights and injuries you may receive, whether they be real or imagined. Instead rejoice that the Lord's permanent record of the redeemed is more than permanent—it is eternal.

So Let It Be Written—
So Let It Be Done

The title words were spoken by Yul Brynner playing Pharaoh Raamses II to Charlton Heston's Moses in the screen epic, "The Ten Commandments." "So let it be written—so let it be done" has become one of the great quotes in all of cinematic history. In my officership I have used that line from time to time in various board and corps council meetings when we have arrived at unanimous agreement on a project. As the secretary enters the recommendation into the minutes, I can't resist evoking the memory of Egyptian royalty with a hearty, "So let it be written—so let it be done."

There is great power in the written word. In those days, once the Pharaoh's verbal command was committed to written form, it had the full and binding force of law without benefit of judicial appeal. In our computer–dependent, information–driven society, we seem to have lost the ability to communicate by writing. I am impressed by the level of sophisticated writing skills our elders had several generations ago when they could not make a quick phone call or pop a note into a fax machine. People from all walks of life faithfully kept extensive diaries that provide for succeeding generations a detailed history of the large and small events that shaped their lives. Letters and journals were family treasures to be read, reread and passed on to future generations. Try doing that to a quickly scribbled sticky note!

I always try to make sure that I communicate good news and encouragement even when I write business letters, because letters last and can be reviewed over and over again. Bad news and correction should be committed to paper only as an absolutely last resort, for once the words are written down they too can be reread many times, building impenetrable walls of resentment and bitterness. There may be times, though, when it is necessary to put the correspondence in writing to make sure that the meaning of the words cannot be confused. Verbal communication can be recalled differently each time it is recounted. Written words remain as they were crafted.

Scripture records all manner of things for our benefit—encouragement, affection, rebuke, instruction, data, prophecy, warnings and promises. The book of Numbers is a comprehensive inventory of pre–Promised Land Israel. I appreciate the fact that the Lord gave writers the task of putting this down on parchment for my benefit. The little book of 1 John tells us that "These things are written so that you may know that you have eternal life" (1 John 5:13). John writes not so you may hope, think or wish, but so you may know that you have eternal life. Choosing salvation through faith in Jesus Christ is the most important choice any of us will ever make.

If someone asks if I am married, I say yes. Not just because I was there at the wedding, but because it is a matter of public and legal record. (Besides that, my wife would clobber me if I forgot.) If people ask about our child, I say that she is ours, and that is verifiable by consulting the legal record listing me as her father. In neither case do I have to guess or make up conclusions. The legal documents establish the fact of the relationships.

The same holds true for your house or car. If it is yours, your name is on the deed. If the car is yours, your name is on the title. Until it is paid for, the bank's name is retained. On that glorious day when the car is paid for, free and clear, there is great rejoicing as the name of the rightful owner is proudly imprinted on the registration. The car may be a dented, rusted, gas–guzzling, oil–burning refugee from the auto graveyard, but it is yours—and you have the title to prove it.

Why then should a person who has confessed their sin, asked the Lord Jesus to be their Savior, and believed that He has done it, be confused over whether or not they are saved? John tells us that "this is written so that you may know that you have eternal life."

Jesus' name is on the record of the transaction; my all—with my sin, weakness, failure and misery—for His all equals redemption, a forgiven past, a productive present and a bright future.

If that is the case, "so let it be written—so let it be done." We can be saved and know it for fact in our own hearts because God wrote it down. And if He wrote it—go out and live it!

How's Your Sole?

It is always fascinating to watch the Lord at work as He breaks into the mundane tasks and situations of life. He presents ministry opportunities galore if we pay attention.

One day I took my uniform shoes to the repair shop to get a new set of heels. It was one of the rare times during a work week that I was not in uniform advertising my ecclesiastical occupation.

"Yes, sir. What can I do for you?" came the cheerful inquiry.

"Just a new set of heels for my shoes, please," I replied.

She examined the shoes and asked quite innocently, "Just heels? How's your sole?"

I don't think she was prepared for my response to such a loaded theological question when I answered, "Fine. Thanks for asking."

She gave me a quizzical look as if to beg for some clarification. "Fine," I continued, "the sole on the bottom of my shoe and the soul God gave me."

During the course of an average week a corps officer is asked thousands of questions. Some have to do with business, staff, finance, procedure, policy and the flow of work at the corps. Others involve spiritual concerns and corps programs. Still others deal with general information: Can The Salvation Army come pick up my old sofa? Do you know the number for the gas company? What time are you picking me up for Home League? This lady has been picked up at the same time for four years and the answer is the same each week. How are your folks? How 'bout those Mets?

All of these are legitimate questions, and each deserves a suitable answer. But beyond the basic information inquiries—how are you, how do you like where you are stationed, how's the family—it has been a long time since someone asked about my soul's health and well–being.

I realize that many questions such as "How are you?" are merely conversational protocol, and few of us expect a genuine response. We have already begun to formulate our reply even as we are making the query. It is just a starter question and not a serious investigation into a person's physical and emotional state.

There are times when we need to ask how a person is in their soul, not in an accusing way but out of a sincere desire to help. We need to ask with the same innocence and sincerity as the girl who asked about my shoes. Paul says to be ready in season and out of season—when it's scheduled and when it's not, to share a word about Jesus and inquire after a person's spiritual well–being. Maybe our inquiry will be the only opportunity they will have to hear and respond to the gospel.

I am glad when people who care about me ask, "How's your soul?" Not to press me, but to allow me to think and experience the conviction of the Holy Spirit. It gives me opportunity to see my need for salvation and growth and make an adult response to Jesus Christ, rather than just finding a quick answer to get the questioner to leave me alone.

Horatio Gates Spafford may have responded to the question this way when reflecting on the pain of the loss of his family who were drowned at sea when their ship went down.

> When peace like a river attendeth my way,
> When sorrows like sea billows roll,
> Whatever my lot, Thou hast taught me to know.
> It is well, it is well with my soul.

> Though Satan should buffet, though trials should come,
> Let this blest assurance control,
> That Christ hath regarded my helpless estate,
> And hath shed His own blood for my soul.

> It is well, with my soul,
> It is well, it is well with my soul.

It is well with my soul—and thanks for asking.

Waltzes with Pigs

One year the Academy awards were dominated by *Dances With Wolves* which won multiple Oscars. The movie gets its title from a soldier who exhibited some bizarre behavior on the frontier by befriending and appearing to dance with a wolf that shared his encampment. The Lakota Sioux Indians in the area were quite amused at his exotic behavior and when they became friends with the soldier they named him "Dances with Wolves."

Scripture records the story of the Prodigal Son (Luke 15) who might be better named "Waltzes with Pigs" for some of his disobedient and disgraceful behavior. Many have heard this story of the brother who begged his father to give him his inheritance early. The boy was sure he could make better decisions than the old man and was quite eager to prove himself in the world. He must have been certain that his father was so old and mentally infirm that he did not have any idea what a young man could accomplish if given freedom of opportunity and adequate resources.

I can well imagine the father doing his best to convince his potentially wayward son of his coming error with logic, emotion, sage advice, anger and a few good "when I was your age" stories. It was not because he begrudged his son the inheritance, for Scripture never indicates that the father was reluctant to give him the money. But the father knew the young man was not prepared for unrestricted adult responsibility. The son had not yet learned how to function outside the boundaries of behavioral limits. So against the father's best parental instincts, the young man got his money—and it was party time.

Luke 15:13 tells us that not long after the young man received his inheritance he spent it on "wild living." We can envision that wild living meant buying rounds of drinks for his so-called friends at every local saloon at every opportunity. It also meant visiting the track, the betting parlors, the casinos and the brothels.

It must have been a wonder to see how popular this young man from the country became and how quickly he fell from that popularity when the money ran out. Once the cash dried up all of his "friends" left him to fend for himself. If he survived—well and good. If not—who cares? Maybe at that point he experienced the first pangs of guilt and knew that his father's advice had been sound.

As if things weren't bad enough, Scripture records that there was a famine in the land. Little food was available at any price. The boy became known as Waltzes with Pigs by his effort to stay alive during a time of famine. This good Jewish boy from a good Jewish family hired himself out to be a keeper of pigs! He probably didn't make any money but was given room and board, which meant a corner of the pigpen and all the slop he could fight from the pigs.

We in the United States have not experienced famine on a wide scale and can only relate to the televised scenes of extreme hunger from places half a world away like Somalia and Ethiopia. Yet just over a century ago, in the midst of the siege of Richmond, Virginia during the Civil War, food became so scarce that a small barrel of flour sold for $250—if you could find it. That is an extraordinary sum of money in 1864 dollars! With hard currency in short supply, people bartered for food using their clothing as their only items of value.

Scripture says the brother "began to be in need" (Luke 15:14, NRSV). It is amazing how quickly starvation sorts out the priorities of life. His free-dom, his recreation, his self–actualization suddenly mattered very little when faced with the prospect of a slow and painful death. I know that young Waltzes with Pigs had no first–hand knowledge of Abraham Maslow's "Hierarchy of Human Needs," which attempts to explain human motives—although I am sure that the aching pain in his stomach took pri-ority over the need for intellectual stimulation. And after sharing his trough with a few defiling porkers, his feeling of self–worth was shot to pieces.

At one point he had been so self–assured that all would be well, but now he was sharing a pigsty with beasts banned as "unclean" under Mosaic Law. If you have ever visited a state fair or a farm show, you will note that swine are not cute little pink pets but enormous, quarter–ton brutes as ill–tempered as they are muddy.

I'm grateful that Jesus' parable of Waltzes with Pigs does not end with him lying face down in the mud, overburdened with guilt and embarrass-ment and at a point of despair where suicide might be preferable to the shame he had brought on himself and his family.

When we come to Jesus, we often find ourselves deep in the muddy mess of our lives. Rebellion lies at the root of our problems; we think that we know better than God. It is only after we realize that we are wrong and that life in the pigsty is no life at all that we are ready to seek Jesus and His plan of redemption.

The Scriptural account reveals that young Waltzes with Pigs woke one day in the midst of the greatest depression of his life. Before deciding to end it all, he had a flash of inspiration to ask his father for forgiveness. He had no hope of being restored to family fellowship but thought to reconstruct his life as one of his father's hired hands. At the very least he could list his newly acquired skill in animal husbandry on his résumé. It must have been a quite a sight to see the young man, covered with mud and reeking of pig droppings stumbling up the road to the family farm. All the while he rehearsed his speech in which he begged for forgiveness and a chance at survival.

Long before Waltzes with Pigs reached the gate, his father saw him and ran to embrace his beloved son who had been returned from death to life. I can picture the son trying to give his practiced speech as his father hugged him and assured him with soft affirmations: "I know, son. It will be all right. I forgive you."

The love of the father had always been there, but the son could not see it until the mud and hunger broke his reckless pride, forcing open his heart and mind. The love of God the Father, as shown in His Son Jesus Christ, was there all the time for us as well. Theologians call it prevenient grace, but we just see it as love—love that draws us from the hunger, mud, shame and bitterness of sin to a glorious homecoming. The message of welcome and forgiveness is there for us—"Get out of the pigpen of sin and come home to Jesus."

Bad to
the Bone

God's word is fair. It shows people at their best and at their worst and the difference is always clear. A classic hard rock song by George Thorogood and the Destroyers speaks of a person who is so bad, he is said to be "bad to the bone."

> Now on the day I was born
> The nurses all gathered around
> And gazed in wide wonder
> At the joy they had found.
> Now the head nurse spoke up,
> "Leave this one alone,"
> She could tell right away
> That I was bad to the bone.

"Bad to the bone" means that rebellion, wickedness and all the rest penetrates to the innermost part of a life. The rebellion is so deep that it forms the framework of an entirely malevolent personality.

When Jesus taught about the kingdom of God, He was approachable and accessible to all people—good and bad. But unlike other religious leaders of the day, Jesus declared that salvation was not a matter of being good but of being forgiven from sin. By that definition, many "nice" people will never know the forgiveness of Jesus Christ if they are trusting only in their own goodness.

In the Sermon on the Mount, Jesus pointed to the Pharisees and said to the assembled crowd, "I tell you that unless your righteousness surpasses that of the Pharisees and teachers of the law, you will certainly not enter the kingdom of heaven" (Matt. 5:21).

These semi–fanatical rule watchers were the all–time award winners of righteousness by good works. They slavishly adhered to a set of minute legal requirements. If we have to be better than they are, what chance do regular, working people have to enter the kingdom of God?

If salvation is based on our good works and adherence to rules, we have no chance. It is impossible to be good enough, for sin makes us "bad to the bone." Paul says the same thing in Ephesians 2:8–9: "For it is by grace you have been saved, through faith—and this not from yourselves, it is the gift of God—not by works, so that no one can boast." You can't ever be good enough to be worthy of heaven, forgiveness or sharing in the holy nature of God. The only thing we are worthy of is God's judgment. But grace is the free, unmerited favor of God that can never be earned or repaid.

In the crucifixion account, Jesus was put to death between two criminals (see Luke 23:32). These criminals were being executed for their crimes—robbery, murder, insurrection, arson or some other equally evil deed—according to law. But the more I study the story, the stranger it gets. The wealthy and influential Romans in those days owned slaves to do their bidding, especially the hard, back–breaking tasks. Good, useful slave laborers were worth a great deal of money. You did not waste good, cheap, disposable manpower by putting them to death. They would no more waste a good slave than we would drive a Rolls Royce in a demolition derby.

If the two felons on the crosses were thieves, why not cut off a hand to teach them a lesson? Weren't they at least strong enough and expendable enough to be chained to an oar on a galley or condemned to hard labor in the copper mines of the Sinai?

The only thing I can imagine is that these two were so wicked that they were beyond rehabilitation or perpetual incarceration. They were so evil as to pose such a threat to life and property that they could not live even in a slave society. They must have been "bad to the bone" and then some.

One of the criminals next to Jesus shouted over the din, "Aren't You the Christ? Save Yourself and us." The other replied with uncharacteristic penitence given their fate and their arrest history, "Don't you fear God, since you are under the same sentence? We are punished justly, for what our deeds deserve. But this man has done nothing wrong." He continued, "Jesus, remember me when You come into Your kingdom."

And Jesus replied, "I tell you the truth, today you will be with Me in paradise" (Luke 23:39–43).

Jesus' words, spoken through His pain, help us understand the context and application of Hebrews 4:12: "For the Word of God is living and active. Sharper than any double–edged sword, it penetrates even to dividing soul and spirit, joints and marrow; it judges the thoughts and attitudes of the heart." In the case of the penitent thief, it was a heart eager for forgiveness.

If you and I are, in fact, "bad to the bone," God's grace and redemption go even deeper!

Revenge Is a Dish Best Served Cold

Our society says "don't get mad—get even." But a Christian should consider a different option based on the ancient Klingon proverb, "Revenge is a dish best served cold."

Our response to provocation should be governed by a calmer attitude than revenge. Scripture does not say we should never be angry but to make sure we do not sin. Be angry at the proper time for the proper reason, but never let it burn inside, leading to sinful retaliation.

The Bible records an incident in 1 Samuel 25 in which David almost made an anger–driven mistake that could have ruined his future leadership of Israel. David, the king–elect living on the run from demented King Saul, spent an entire season helping a herder named Nabal to protect his sheep from predators—four–legged and two–legged.

After performing this extra duty, David sent men to Nabal to ask for food and comfort as the shearing celebration drew near. But Nabal refused and treated David's messengers with extreme disrespect and crudeness. Although a man of considerable wealth, Nabal was an ignorant, unreasonable lout. Fortunately, he was married to a gracious and courageous woman. Abigail managed to defuse this potentially explosive situation.

David was never one to back down from a fight. No one would ever insult him and live to brag about it. He erupted with rage and was ready to kill Nabal and his entire family in revenge.

Abigail knew what needed to be done to cool David's anger while still remaining loyal to her spouse. As soon as she heard of her husband's foolishness, she and her household staff prepared a feast for David and his men. Hoping to halt a vendetta with some good homecooking, she prepared 200 loaves of bread, two skins of wine, five butchered sheep, a bushel of roasted grain, 100 cakes of raisins and 200 cakes of pressed figs. This may be the first mention of Fig Newtons served by the Bible's first caterer.

Abigail met David along the trail and humbly fell at his feet pleading, "My lord, let the blame be on me alone ... May my lord pay no attention to that wicked man Nabal. He is just like his name—his name is 'Fool' ...

But as for me, your servant, I did not see the men my master sent" (1 Sam. 25:24).

Abigail took responsibility for the breach of hospitality and urged David to consider his actions. She was as concerned for her family as she was for the future king of Israel, since she did not want him to be marked by an act of savagery that would taint his reign forever. She said, "Since the Lord has kept you, my master, from bloodshed and from avenging yourself with your own hands, ... let this gift, which your servant has brought to my master, be given to the men who follow you. Please forgive your servant's offense ..." (1 Sam. 25:26–28).

David was deeply impressed by both her loyalty and her wisdom in protecting the integrity and reputation of the future king. Returning home Abigail informed her semi–drunken husband how close he had come to being killed for his stupidity. He was so shocked that he had a stroke and died ten days later. It is no wonder that when David heard that bit of news, he quickly proposed to Abigail to make her one of his wives. Had David acted in the heat of his anger, his kingship might have been ruined. Abigail helped to cool David's rage so he could consider his actions and their possible repercussions. And like cold leftovers, revenge lost its appeal.

"Do not repay anyone evil for evil. Be careful to do what is right in the eyes of everybody ... Do not take revenge ... Do not be overcome by evil, but overcome evil with good" (Rom. 12:17,19, 21). So when a driver cuts you off, or someone insults you or treats you badly, retaliate with kindness. And in our crazy world, that will make news: "Man performs random act of kindness—film at 11:00 ..."

You Can't Hide
Your Lyin' Eyes

It is amazing how sins we thought were well hidden have a habit of coming back to haunt us, even when we have covered our tracks and left no witnesses. Our sins have no fibers, hair, blood, DNA or fingerprints, but they still have a way of making our lives miserable until God deals with them.

On the way to the Promised Land the Israelites were commanded to defeat the fortified city of Jericho. Since the entire city was to be an offering to God, no one was allowed to take any souvenirs. This would help them remember to trust the Lord to supply all their needs and to be obedient to His commands. They could not afford to break either of those standards—trust and obedience—and hope to live in harmony with God. They all knew better. Or so it seemed.

The Bible tells us that Jericho was defeated just as God promised (Josh. 6). But a short time later, when Joshua sent a small detachment to fight the city of Ai, they were defeated.

"Lord, what is happening?" Joshua cried. "Why did You leave us?"

The Lord told him that one of the Israelites had flagrantly disobeyed Him by looting forbidden goods from Jericho. That sin had to be confronted before the Lord would do any more for them.

Joshua commanded all the people to assemble, and by lot of the 12 tribes he picked Judah. Of that tribe he picked the clan of the Zerahites, the family of Zimri and finally he picked Achan. Joshua singled him out from the entire population of hundreds of thousands of people—talk about a needle in a haystack!

"My son," Joshua ordered. "Give glory to the Lord, the God of Israel, and give Him the praise. Tell me what you have done; do not hide it from me" (Josh. 7:19).

"I did it," said Achan. "I have sinned against God. When I saw a beautiful robe from Babylon and big chunks of silver and gold I went crazy. I knew it was wrong, but it was more wealth than I had ever seen, right there for the taking. So I took it and buried it under my tent, and it is there right now."

A quick search revealed it was right where Achan said.

"Why have you brought this disaster on us, Achan?" He asked. "Why did you do this thing when you knew it was wrong?

How did Joshua know what Achan had done? How did the others know? Maybe the song by the Eagles is more true than we imagine.

You can't hide your lyin' eyes
And your smile is a thin disguise
Thought by now you'd realize,
There ain't no way to hide your lyin' eyes.

As a result Achan—along with his entire family—were stoned to death. Then all their possessions were cremated and buried as a permanent reminder of the danger of disobedience. Because nothing happened right away, Achan thought he had gotten away with it. But sin always has a way of coming back to trip us up. The result might not be as dramatic as Achan's situation, but lies, deceptions and "small" sins corrupt our best efforts and damage the harmony of a close relationship with God.

Numbers 32:23 is just as true for us as for the ancients: "You may be sure that your sin will find you out." Before a God who knows our hearts we can't hide our lyin' eyes. But we can praise God that 1 John 1:9 is also true: "If we confess our sins, He [God] is faithful and just and will forgive us our sins and purify us from all unrighteousness."

Blessed Insurance

During an open air service, one summer cadet who came from Puerto Rico led the favorite old hymn, "Blessed Assurance."

> Blessed assurance, Jesus is mine;
> O what a foretaste of glory divine!
> Heir of salvation, purchase of God,
> Born of His spirit, washed in His blood.
>
> This is my story, this is my song,
> Praising my Savior all the day long.
>
> (Fanny Crosby)

But since his fluency in English was a rather new acquisition, the lyrics of the song came out, "Blessed *insurance*, Jesus is mine ..." But now that I think about it, he may be on to something.

People make insurance premium payments for many years expecting a reasonable, safe return on their investment. They want to provide retirement income, or survivor benefits or to ensure their family's financial security in case of accident. Unfortunately, insurance companies can fall on hard times when the anticipated return on investment portfolios do not materialize. They may have to reduce annuity payments or limit the opportunity to redeem the policies. In some worst cases, insurance companies must cancel coverage completely.

Insurance is bought in anticipation of future need. If we buy a VCR, a boat, or a washing machine, we expect to use it as soon as we get home from the store. We would not think of paying for an item we would never use. Insurance, whether for life, health, auto or home owner protection is paid in anticipation of future need. Someday when—not if, but when—I have an accident, get sick, retire, or die, there will be resources available for me and my loved ones. We hope we will never need to file a claim but we know we are providing for the day when the inevitable crisis comes crashing into the security of our daily existence. Payments on an insurance policy just don't bring the same enjoyment as does a major purchase we have saved and planned for, but they do provide a certain sense of well–being.

We worry about our financial security and wonder what will happen to our families when we can no longer provide for them. We should be concerned about our spiritual security as well.

Jesus told a parable about a man who was obsessed with acquisition and finances. He built barns to hold his immense harvest and pulled them down to build bigger barns in anticipation of storing and enjoying his fortune. In the process he neglected his relationship with God. He is called the Rich Fool because he died without enjoying the benefit of his financial planning.

The Lord reminded those listening to the parable, "Provide purses for yourselves that will not wear out, a treasure in heaven that will not be exhausted, where no thief comes near and no moth destroys. For where your treasure is, there your heart will be also" (Luke 12:33–34).

Jesus said that the real treasure of the heart was not to be found in acquisition of possessions or the accumulation of wealth, but in having a personal relationship with God. "The fruit of righteousness will be peace; the effect of righteousness will be quietness and confidence forever." The turmoil of guilt and sin has been settled and our future is secure.

Maybe Paul had the right idea concerning "blessed insurance" when he wrote, "For I am persuaded that He [Jesus] is able to keep that which I have committed unto Him against that day" [the day of Christ's return or our demise—whichever comes first] (1 Tim. 1:12). He stated that he had committed everything of value to the Lord, his past, present and future. We can do the same by committing our family, our work and our relationships into the Lord's care and keeping. God will never cancel the policy or break His eternal promises. That puts our lives in God's hands—and His hands are better than any insurance that Allstate or anyone else has to offer.

Win or Lose ...
You Have to Choose

While walking down the street I passed a young man who wore a dirty, black tee shirt imprinted with the word "Loser." Shirts are a walking commentary on society as they record sports teams, schools and places visited. The only one I do not appreciate is the one that reads, "I'm with Stupid" and an arrow is pointed in my direction. But a shirt with the single word "Loser" is not only unusual, it is painful.

We may feel like that at times, but we work diligently to conceal our weaknesses and hurts and try to market our best selves. We keep up a courageous front even when we are falling apart inside.

Our modern, win–at–all–cost society has no tolerance for losers. The silver medal means you are only second rate. The Bible speaks of losers. Adam and Eve fouled up a perfect relationship with God in an ideal setting. Their son Cain was the first murderer and their other son Abel the first victim. Jacob cheated his brother out of his inheritance. Jacob's sons sold their brother Joseph into slavery. King David was an adulterer and an accessory to murder. In a moment of testing, Peter lied that he ever knew Jesus. And the list of potential losers goes on and on.

These days it is quite fashionable to make the transition from loser to victim. A victim can always use abuse, injury, circumstance or disappointment, real or imagined, as a rationale for failure or bizarre behavior. Defendants in our courts use the so–called "victim defense." The rationale goes something like this: "I may have shot you 36 times, but that was because I had a bad Sunday School teacher."

I heard one person use the victim defense concerning his weight. The husband said, "It is my mother's fault. She fed me too well. Actually, I'm not really overweight—I'm big boned." His wife replied, "If you were any more big–boned you could be in the museum's Hall of Dinosaurs!"

Some folks are truly scarred by the horrible things they have experienced, and for them I have great compassion. But others take the role of victim to eliminate responsibility for their lives and actions. They say, "It is not my fault. I'd like to be better, but I can't—so I won't."

Scripture relates the truth that losers and victims can become winners

(Acts 3:1–10). The man crippled from birth who made his living begging by the Temple gate in Jerusalem was brought in by his friends. Dressed in his "Loser" shirt, he begged for handouts. Being a smart beggar, he didn't expect too much from businessmen and commuters. That is why he staked out his favorite begging spot by the Temple where people might tend to be more generous after a time of prayer and thanksgiving.

As Peter and John came through the gate, he sized them up as good donor prospects and gave them his best pitch. "Please sirs, see what has happened to me. It wasn't my fault ... I have nothing ... I'm a loser ... won't you please give me some spare change?"

I doubt if the beggar was prepared for what happened next. Rather than tossing a few coins into his cup, Peter and John stopped to talk to him.

"Look at us," Peter said, not as a request but as an order.

"Oh good," the beggar thought. "Surely these guys will be generous and I can go home early today."

"Silver and gold I do not have," Peter said, "but what I have I give you."

"All right," the beggar thought, "maybe a sandwich or a jacket or a little wine to get me through the night. Anything would be good."

"In the name of Jesus of Nazareth, walk," Peter declared.

"Are you nuts? If I could walk I'd be doing something else. I'm a loser. My parents told me that. My friends told me that. The only thing I have ever been good at is begging. And you want me to walk?"

The beggar could have remained a loser since he was incapable of seeing himself otherwise. He had played the part so long and so well that he was trapped by his flawed perception.

But Peter took him by the hand and helped him up as the man's feet and ankles immediately became stronger. Scripture says that within a matter of moments the man was with Peter and John in the Temple courts, and was "walking and jumping, and praising God" (Acts 3:8).

People recognized him as the same man who sat by the gate day after day, year in and year out begging and acting like a loser. They were astonished by the transformation.

He was probably more amazed than they at what could only be described as a miracle. What started as another average day in a long succession of days as a loser became the most glorious day of his life.

When we first hear of Jesus and the message of grace, we come as losers. We hope to beg for just a little bit of Jesus to help us drag along through life. We know we are losers and victims, and we sometimes try to blame someone else for our situation. Jesus breaks in on our failure and gives us much more than we ever hoped for or expected. He wants to give us forgiveness, grace and a future of hope. He's in the business of changing losers into winners. All we need is to ask and believe.

Which do you want to be—a winner or a loser? You choose.

Isn't It
True?

Watching high profile court cases on television might lead us to think of spiritual things in a trial setting. We stand before God, caught in the act of sin with no possible plea other than "guilty as charged." As Satan prepares his case to corroborate our wickedness, all we can do is throw ourselves on the mercy of the court, as our advocate Jesus Christ speaks on our behalf.

When God sees that His Son speaks for us and we are redeemed by Jesus' death and resurrection, the Righteous Judge hands down His verdict while Satan is still rehearsing his opening statement:

"Guilty as charged—yet this court finds the accused pardoned of all sins, charges and specifications. Case closed, never to be heard again."

Satan, whose name means "the accuser of the brethren," still takes great delight in trying to impeach our testimony of what God has done and is doing in our lives. That is why it is so important that Jesus intercedes with God on our behalf.

When we are confident, faithful, serene and blessed of God, Satan tries to tear down our testimony. He begins his cross–examination:

"We have heard your comments regarding joy in the Lord since you claim to be forgiven from sin. But isn't it true that you yell at other drivers and make disparaging comments about their driving ability? Isn't it true that you sometimes lose your temper?"

"Isn't it true that you told your wife you would fix the sink as soon as the ball game was over and you have not fixed it yet? Isn't it true that you claim to be excited about the Lord's work, but when volunteers are needed for a 7:00 am prayer breakfast you grumble about being too tired? I ask you, where is the supposed joy you claim to have?

"I submit, rather, that as a Christian witness, your testimony is flawed. My cross–examination proves that you do not have joy; you do not have abundant love for others; and you do not have this alleged peace of God. And isn't it true that your life shows little evidence of your love for Jesus at all? You claim to be living to please Jesus when in fact you are weak, imperfect and anything but the joyful Christian warrior you would like to be. Well, what do you have to say for yourself?"

All we can do is quote from the record: "If we claim to be without sin, we deceive ourselves and the truth is not in us. If we confess our sins, He [God] is faithful and just and will forgive us our sins and purify us from all unrighteousness." The Apostle John continues, "My dear children, I write this to you so that you will not sin. But if anybody does sin, we have One who speaks to the Father in our defense—Jesus Christ the Righteous one" (1 John 1:8–9;2:1).

"If there are any questions," we can reply, "I suggest that you speak to my counsel—Jesus Christ. But let me remind you, He has a special relationship with the Judge that always works in favor of the redeemed of God whom you accuse."

There goes the case. We have pleaded guilty to our sin, been convicted of our rebellion against God and claimed the atoning sacrifice of Jesus Christ to pay the price for sin—and rather than clemency, we have received a full pardon.

Born to Be Wild

Almost any Sunday School kid can tell you the story of Samson and Delilah. They know that he got a hair cut, lost his strength and killed all his enemies and himself when he knocked down the pillars of the temple of Dagon.

If we were to pick a specific piece of music that defined Samson's life and personality, it might be "Born to Be Wild." This rock classic by Steppenwolf became the unofficial anthem for the turbulent and rebellious 1960s. If you change the 1960s to ancient Israel during the time of the Judges, and insert the primary character of Samson, "born to be wild" fits quite nicely. Since there was no king in Israel, "everyone did what was right in their own eyes" especially headstrong, self–centered Samson.

> Get your motor runnin'
> Head out on the highway,
> Lookin' for adventure,
> In whatever comes our way.
>
> I like smoke and lightnin'
> Heavy metal thunder
> Racin' with the wind
> and the feeling that I'm under.
>
> Like a true nature's child,
> We were born, born to be wild ...

Following the death of Moses and Joshua, those who reached the promised land soon forgot the Lord's commands. In fact, the Israelites did everything imaginable to rebel against Him. "They forsook the Lord, the God of their fathers, who had brought them out of Egypt ... They provoked the Lord to anger because they forsook Him ... In His anger against Israel the Lord handed them over to raiders who plundered them ... Then the Lord raised up judges who saved them out of the hands of these raiders" (Judg. 2:12–16).

Whenever Israel fell into difficulty, the first thing the people did was pray and plead their case to the Lord. When raided, taxed, oppressed, impressed, depressed, rejected, neglected and disrespected they begged the Lord for help. Maybe it was more whining than true repentance. In His great mercy, God sent judges, or deliverers, to their aid. Of all the deliverers, the most famous was Samson.

As God's man to help Israel, he was born to be different. Instead, he lived as if he was born to be wild.

Judges chapter 13 records the miraculous announcement and nature of his birth in response to his mother's prayer. He was to be a Nazirite (one who made a specific, voluntary promise to serve God) for his entire life. As part of this ritual separation for service, both he and his mother were to abstain from all alcohol and all fermented or dried fruits. They were also forbidden to touch dead bodies. (I am sure the Lord knew about germs and fetal alcohol syndrome long before we thought of it.) And Samson was never to get a haircut. His long hair was not the source of his strength, but rather an outward reminder of the vow and his pledge of obedience to the Lord.

Back in the 1960s, long hair was more than just an expression of fashion and independence. Our parents hated it, and we loved to watch them hating it. Samson loved to show off and do whatever he pleased, even if his parents hated it. I can picture Samson, a large tattoo on his arm reading "Born to be Wild," astride a Harley Davidson chopper, with a good-looking Philistine girl seated behind him. His long hair would be flying in the wind, since he wasn't the type to obey helmet laws. And through it all, I can almost hear the anguished cries of his mother and father.

"Samson, the Lord gave you to us as an answer to prayer. We have cared for you and done everything a parent could do. And now you go and break our hearts and shame us by your stupid antics?"

"When are you going to grow up, Samson? You are a Nazirite for the Lord and for Israel, and all you do is pick fights with the Philistines and hang out with the wrong crowd.

"You are bright and good-looking, and you are wasting your life. All you want to do is party and fight, party and fight. If I've told you once, I've told you a thousand times to grow up, settle down, marry a nice Jewish girl, and do what you know is right! Don't be such a jerk, Samson!"

You know the story of Samson's fall. Delilah nagged and toyed with him until he came close to revealing the truth. As long as he hinted that the strength was in the ropes or the way in which he was bound, he was safe.

But once Samson began to touch upon things sacred, his hair and his promises to God, he was in serious trouble.

"Samson, if you love me ... tell me," Delilah whined. He eventually gave in and look what happened—he got a crew cut, lost his eyes and became a public joke to be ridiculed by the Philistine oppressors. Fortunately, he managed to get in one last shot for the Lord. While he was serving as the power source for the local grain–grinding establishment, he had plenty of time to pray and repent. When Samson realized that his strength was increasing in direct proportion to the stubble on his scalp, he knew that he needed to use those physical powers for one last valiant gesture as judge of Israel. The last bit of super–human power made it possible for Samson to topple the temple of Dagon. Unfortunately, Samson was crushed along with his enemies.

Scripture states in Samson's obituary in Judges 16:31 that "he had led Israel 20 years." It seems a great waste of ability and opportunity that he led Israel for such a short period of time. He died just when he should have been in his prime of strength, judgment and wisdom.

Samson was dedicated to the Lord's work and born to be God's man. Instead he behaved as though he was "born to be wild." In a similar way we are given opportunities and abilities from God, and He will hold us accountable for what we do with His gifts. Samson had grown up willful to the point that his parents could no longer influence him for good. He may have been the prototypical child that Solomon wrote about: "Even a child is known by his actions, by whether his conduct is pure and right ... The rod of correction imparts wisdom, but a child left to himself disgraces his mother" (Prov. 20:11; 29:15).

Paul wrote some good advice to another young man who could have grown up to be wild. He told his friend and protégé Timothy: "Don't let anyone look down on you because you are young, but set an example for the believers in speech, in life, in love, in faith and in purity. Do not neglect your gift. Be diligent in these matters; give yourself wholly to them. Watch your life and doctrine closely. Persevere in them, because if you do, you will save yourself and your hearers" (1 Tim. 4:11–12; 14–16).

We can only wonder what Samson's life might have produced if he had lived as God's man rather than as if he were born to be wild. Samson's way ended in death; Timothy's in life and ministry for Jesus over a long and useful career. I think I like Timothy's way better, don't you?

Maybe We Should Try the Slogan Backwards?

While attending a church growth and leadership conference, we learned the importance of providing slogans or catchy phrases that keep the church's mission before the congregation. The Salvation Army has been blessed with some of the finest slogans ever devised like "Heart to God and Hand to Man."

That little phrase succinctly states the Army's goals in first giving our worship to God and then practical service to His creation. It has served well for many years to keep the vision and the mission before the Army and before those who support its programs and services. Yet over the years we have moaned and groaned that people readily see the Army as a powerful social service provider, but not as a church. If we have promoted the portion that speaks of "hand to man" without sharing the ministry that begins with our "heart to God," that is our fault not theirs.

Have we repeated the slogan so often that it has ceased to have any meaning? It would be tragic if the symbol came to have a greater importance than what it represented. Perhaps it might be profitable to examine the slogan in reverse—"Hands to God and Heart to man."

It might be good to start with our hand in God's hand. All of Scripture from Genesis to Revelation deals with God's planning and execution of His grand plan to bring us back to holiness and fellowship, to be what He created us to be before sin ruined us. This is often called "our way to God." All of the recorded advances, setbacks, trials and victories, including the ultimate victory of Jesus Christ, served to bring us back to a loving God: "For God so loved the world that He gave His one and only Son, that whoever believes in Him shall not perish but have eternal life" (John 3:16).

Not only does He love us, for that is what we would want God to do, but He *likes* us as well. God likes us so much that He could not bear the thought of spending eternity without us.

The Bible deals with another great truth. Not only is God interested in making us right positionally as far as our redemption is concerned, He wants us to live right relationally as well. The rest of Scripture calls this "our walk with God," and it is this walk that is most pleasing to God. "He has shown you, O man, what is good. And what does the Lord require of you? To act justly and to love mercy and to walk humbly with your God" (Mic. 6:8).

1 John 1:6–7 tells us to "walk in the light as He is in the light." Even if you do not notice all the theological metaphors of light (righteousness) and darkness (sin and rebellion), it is best to walk with the Lord because He knows where all the stumps and holes are. If we have His hand, we won't trip or get lost by wandering away on our own.

When walking with God or anyone we love, it is important that we go together. I like to walk with my wife—not ahead or behind but hand in hand, arm in arm. Not only is it nice to be close to her, but it makes it possible to hold a conversation without having to shout with the entire neighborhood listening in! Walking together is even more important when it comes to small children. As a responsible, loving father, I would not cross the street ahead of my child and then wave her across. I would hold her securely by the hand, making sure she is safe and protected from danger as she crosses with me.

We desire to please God with our zeal and creativity, but we lack the perseverance to walk patiently with the Lord. God just takes too long to get on our schedule. As a result, we dream dreams and scheme schemes and then ask the Lord to bless them after the fact. In many cases we ask the Lord to bless these dreams and schemes after we have made a mess of them. We pray that He will swoop in and make everything right before we get any deeper into trouble.

We pray, "Lord, we have a problem." But the Lord replies, "We? No my friend. You have a problem. It was never My idea, My plan or My way. You took it upon yourself to run on ahead rather than walk along with Me. It won't be My problem unless you and I are in this together."

King David thought it would be a good idea to number all the fighting men in Israel, even though the Lord told him not to because God wanted to be Israel's power and protection. God wanted them to trust in Him rather than depending on the size of their army.

David proceeded with his headcount, in spite of God's wishes, and 2 Samuel 24 records the consequences. David did not "walk humbly with his God." He ran ahead and made his own plans and relied on his own efforts. Perhaps David thought that God would somehow overlook disobedience and presumption and make everything work out anyway. He did not do that for David any more than He does it for us.

God allowed David to choose the method of his punishment. Of the options presented—three years of famine, three months of running from his enemies, or three days of plague—David chose the three days of plague. For his failure to walk with God and listen to His advice, "the Lord sent a plague on Israel from that morning until the end of the time designated, and 70,000 of the people from Dan to Beersheba died" (2 Sam. 24:15).

The prophet Jeremiah recorded another occurence of disobedience. In Jeremiah 2:27, the Lord is saddened by Israel's allegiance to false idols: "They have turned their backs to me and not their faces; yet when they are in trouble, they say, Come and save us!" How often do we choose to go our own way and then want the Lord to rescue us from ourselves and our arrogance? It is difficult to walk close together when all the Lord sees is our backs as we race on ahead of Him.

If we are walking hand–in–hand with the Lord, it will be impossible for us to stray from His direction. We will be so close that we can hear His voice and gain strength from His presence.

Once we are walking hand–in–hand with God, we are in a position to give our heart to people in need of material assistance and much more. A food order, a bed for the night or a "cup of cold water" is good for the short term, but what about the deep inner needs: freedom from guilt; affirmation and belonging in a lonely, uncaring world; a sense of purpose?

We spend millions of dollars for food, shelter and counseling in the hope that people will translate a newfound belief in Jesus Christ into responsible living. It doesn't happen automatically. We need to give away the physical resources without neglecting to offer the one thing that gives our ministry credibility—our hearts.

Giving away our hearts feeds souls hungry for purpose. It feeds the hungry and needy of emotional and spiritual nourishment, as well as feeding those hungry in stomach. Giving away our hearts completes the command of Micah 6:8; we have "acted justly" and "loved mercy," or demonstrated kindness as we "walk humbly with our God."

Giving our hearts away also settles the integrity issue currently plaguing the Church. Our interest is not in funding, for if we are walking hand–in–hand with the Lord, He will take care of the plan and the money. Our interest is not in public relations. We are more concerned with what God thinks of us than what the public thinks. And our interest is not in making people dependent or obligated to us, or getting them to attend church for what they can get rather than for what they can give.

Giving our hearts fulfills the command to "Go and make disciples," giving of ourselves and sharing what Jesus can and will do for those who ask Him.

Our challenge is to walk with the Lord and open our hearts as His servants with "our hand in God's hand, and our hearts to man." Then we will see a return on our ministry investment that will bear eternal dividends.

Who Do You Say That I Am?

What would the press have said about Jesus? If pollsters could have measured Jesus' popularity, how would He have fared? Perhaps it is good that Jesus came when He did. Otherwise, He might not have accomplished much in His three years of ministry with reporters and photographers hovering nearby to record everything He said or did.

I can imagine the comments if Jesus were to come back today and perform the equivalent of upsetting the money changers' tables at the Temple or chastising the Pharisees as "blind guides" and "whitewashed tombs full of dead bones." The news media might brand Him a lunatic or an intolerant "phobe" of some variety.

"Who does Jesus think He is, telling people that their sins are forgiven?" they might report. "Healing people is wonderful, as long as it doesn't get out of hand. How will the medical industry survive if Jesus keeps healing people? Jesus' message has severe implications for the global economy."

They might quote Jesus' words: "No one comes to the Father except through Me" (John 14:6) and brand Him a megalomaniac. Next, the media might do an in–depth investigative report. "Tonight, 'Jesus of Nazareth—Deity or Deception?'" I wonder how the news might have reported the Resurrection—"Raised or Ruse?—film at 11." It makes you think.

Thomas Carlyle said, "If Jesus were to come today, people would not even crucify Him. They would ask Him to dinner and hear what He had to say, and make fun of it." TV talk shows would interview Him and laugh Him off as they went to commercial. Investigative reporters would eagerly dig up anything they could possibly find on Jesus, not to verify His claims, but to find something to be used against Him. "He was such a good kid. Quiet ... never caused any trouble." But that is what they have reported about mad bombers and mass murderers.

Jesus would likely run afoul of nearly every government agency or regulatory group. The Bureau of Alcohol, Tobacco and Firearms might protest His changing water to wine at Cana without a license, or the Sierra Club might disparage the miraculous—though excessive and potentially out of season—catch of fish. The Weather Channel might be upset every time

Jesus calmed a storm, while the Coast Guard could berate Him for walking on water without wearing an approved flotation device!

The Pharisees were most definitely anti–Jesus. By their own admission, if Jesus were allowed to continue His ministry unchecked, the Romans would take away their position of authority. Yet everywhere Jesus went, huge crowds followed, desperately seeking His help. They had been to the "experts," and none of them had any remedy.

Some could tell how they had been blind but could now see, or lame and could now walk. A young man who had been diagnosed as insane could testify to perfect mental health. And Lazarus could tell how he had been dead—not clinically dead or nearly dead, but totally dead—complete with death certificate, flowers and hearse.

But I doubt if the news media would be interested. They might get a statement from the funeral directors' association to report on the negative impact raising the dead would have on their profession. The Pharisees might ask by what right Jesus presumed to decide who lives and who dies? "Who does He think He is—God?"

Well, yes, He does, because He is!

Jesus reminded them that many are "ever seeing but never perceiving, and ever hearing but never understanding otherwise they might turn and be forgiven" (Mark 4:12).

Accepting Jesus is an individual decision not based on public opinion. When a seeking heart cuts through the barrage of information, God performs wonderful miracles of discovery. A jailer in Philippi in the midst of a jailbreak asks, "What must I do to be saved?" (Acts 16:30) and understands. A woman from Samaria with questionable morals meets Jesus and discovers that He is the Messiah.

When Jesus came to the region of Caesarea Philippi, He asked His disciples, "Who do people say the Son of Man is?"

They replied, "Some say John the Baptist; others say Elijah; and still others, Jeremiah or one of the prophets."

"But what about you?" He asked. "Who do you say I am?"

Simon Peter answered, "You are the Christ, the Son of the living God."

Jesus replied, "Blessed are you, Simon son of Jonah, for this was not revealed to you by man, but by My Father in heaven" (Matt. 16:13–17).

You will have to answer that same question for yourself without benefit of a poll or survey. "Who do you say that Jesus is?"

Isaiah lists many of His names, none of which are on a poll or news survey: "And He will be called Wonderful Counselor, Mighty God,

Everlasting Father, Prince of Peace" (Isa. 9:6).

Know Him as Savior and Lord. Know the freedom that comes from being forgiven from sin and being transformed into His holy character.

Read the
Fine Print

In our litigation–crazed society, companies and manufacturers are careful not to make any claims or guarantees that might not hold up in court. They always put some form of standard disclaimer or caution in their advertising or on the product to protect them from a lawsuit.

For example, your state Department of Transportation does not install "guard rails" any more. Now they are called "guide rails"—to guide your car back onto the highway. They dropped "guard" since it implies a more significant level of protection.

"Waterproof" watches are now "water resistant." Since no one can be absolutely certain that a timepiece will never leak, there is potential for a liability suit.

What parent hasn't spent hours in careful preparation for Christmas morning, only to see too late those three horrible little words—"batteries not included."

Here are a few others that you may recognize: "Suggested manufacturer's list price for the new Turbo charged LZX 5000 is $27,500—excluding title, tax and dealer prep; The LZX 5000's fuel efficiency is rated at 52 miles per gallon highway, 12 in the city ... Your mileage may vary."

Some disclaimers are really warnings, like "close cover before striking" or "do not puncture or incinerate." Once a friend who was working with a can of spray paint decided to put a small hole in the top of the can to help the heavy paint escape easier. Did it ever! It exploded straight up all over his kitchen ceiling!

Or how about the disclaimer found on all medicines: "Use only as directed." A man at the corps thought that if taking two tablets every four hours was good—four tablets every two hours would be even better! He isn't with us anymore. He forgot the instruction of Proverbs 19:16, "He who obeys instructions guards his soul, but he who is contemptuous of his ways will die."

The results of inattention are not always so tragic, but can still be quite memorable. We have a friend who once accidentally brushed her teeth with Ben–Gay. She will never do that again.

There are other warnings such as "any rebroadcasts of the descriptions and accounts of this game without the expressed permission of Major League Baseball are strictly prohibited." So be careful what you talk about at the watercooler, unless you have permission.

Throughout Scripture Jesus spoke to real people about real needs and genuine matters of life and death. None of it was done purely for intellectual stimulation. Jairus needed help for his little girl; lepers needed healing; Bartimaus wanted to see, and Nicodemus desperately wanted to know that he could have eternal life. No disclaimer intersperses the Scripture such as can be found at the end of a movie credit: "all of the events and characters portrayed are fictional and any similarity to events and people living or dead is purely coincidental."

Jesus' promises contain no disclaimers to give Him an "out." He gave good news to tired, beat up, burned out people: "Come to Me ... and I will give you rest" (Matt. 11:28). He encouraged rejected, disappointed, abused and lonely people: "Surely I am with you always, to the very end of the age" (Matt. 28:20).

He made a promise to those without a place to belong in this world: "Do not let your hearts be troubled. Trust in God; trust also in Me. In My Father's house are many rooms ... I am going there to prepare a place for you ... that you also may be where I am" (John 14:1–4).

Jesus made an inviolable promise to the penitent thief who asked Jesus to remember him: "Today you will be with Me in paradise" (Luke 23:43).

The Lord is always faithful to His promises, and you will never find in them fine print or a disclaimer. All who have accepted Jesus as Savior are deeply grateful that John 3:16 reads, "For God so loved the world that He gave His one and only Son, that whoever believes in Him shall not perish but have eternal life," and does not end with "offer void where prohibited."

The Lord Knows
How to Celebrate

Heaven is a wonderful place,
Filled with glory and grace.
I'm gonna see my Savior's face,
'Cause heaven is a wonderful, heaven is a glorious,
Heaven is a wonderful place.

We have heard the chorus often since the days of Sunday School and would generally agree that heaven must surely be a wonderful place. Not because of pearly gates or streets of gold, or saints worshipping around the throne of God, but because Jesus is there. He is the One who loved us so much that He became sin for us to restore us to a right relationship with God the Father. He is the One who made it possible for us to have the character of God and to spend eternity with Him in unending fellowship.

Contrary to what some may think, heaven doesn't start when we die. When believers die, they are then ready to inherit all that has been prepared for them. The love relationship that began on earth continues uninterrupted forever. That is heaven.

Those who wanted to stay as far from Jesus Christ as they could in this life will be allowed to stay as far from Him as they desire without hope of release. That is called hell.

But heaven is the goal of every Christian life, because God knows how to celebrate, and He fills His kingdom with joy, just as He fills our lives with joy here.

I don't claim to be an expert on heaven because I have never been there. But I do believe that heaven will have everything to keep us happy and completely satisfied in all areas of our lives forever. It may have baseball and brass bands or some of your favorite things. I'll have unlimited opportunity to see my Christian ancestors, friends in Christ, pastors and teachers. I will want to thank them personally for that ministry because they shared the gospel with me and invited me to know Jesus as Savior.

John's vision in Revelation 4 gives some insight into what heaven looks like. He records bursts of light brighter than anything he had ever seen. He was dazzled by the pure brilliance of the glory of God. It overloaded his senses, making it difficult to describe the indescribable. All he could do was liken the sight to the fire and clarity of precious gemstones. All around the throne were elders, and the saints and angels, dressed in glowing white robes and wearing gold crowns. And there was sound.

To say "there was sound" is to grossly understate. Lightning and thunder came from the One who sat on the throne while all around echoed the sound of singing, worship and praise, "Holy, Holy, Holy, Lord God Almighty—the One who was, and is, and is to come!" (Rev. 4:8).

Scripture also tells us that heaven rejoices more over one sinner who repents than all the saints who think their good deeds will save them. Heaven resounds with cheers and applause each time a soul is won back from sin and hell. Maybe we had better learn to get in a joyful frame of worship, seeing that we will be spending eternity together in praise and celebration. We will celebrate then and now because God knows how—and He is teaching us.

Once at a playoff game my team came back to win the deciding game with the last at bat. It was one of the most exciting finishes I have ever seen. People cheered, laughed, applauded, sang, danced and celebrated a momentary vicarious victory with a refreshing sense of abandon. Businessmen in designer suits hugged burly truck–driver types in worn work clothes and exchanged "high fives" as if they had all shared in the most thrilling moment of history. The elderly lady sitting next to me gave me such a hug that I thought she was going to crush me. I had never experienced 54,000 people celebrating with such exuberance.

A distorted view of God sees Him as one who hates to celebrate. We see Him as a caricature of His true nature, as one who is never satisfied with our performance or commitment.

We see him, as David Seamands illustrates in his book *Putting Away Childish Things,* as a demanding parent who expects more and better each time. He is never pleased and never proud of us as His children. If we work as hard as we possibly can in school and earn a C, why didn't we get a B? And when we work the C to a B with great effort and sacrifice, why didn't we get an A? And when we get that A hoping at last to satisfy our harsh taskmaster by presenting an academic offering to celebrate, the answer comes back, "An A? That teacher must be an easy marker."

Take heart, God knows how to celebrate, and He takes great delight whenever His children reach out to Him. He is a loving Father who knows how to bring out the best as He celebrates our victories with all the saints and angels. His love is never conditional or contingent upon my level of Christian performance, for He loves me even when I fall short. He loves me and made a way for my salvation long before I even knew the first thing about God.

Jesus reminds us how much He loved us: "Which of you, if his son asks for bread, will give him a stone? Or if he asks for a fish, will give him a snake? If you then, though you are evil, know how to give good gifts to your children, how much more will your Father in heaven give good gifts to those who ask Him!" (Matt. 7:9–11). Not only does the Lord know how to give perfect gifts, He knows how to rejoice in the spiritual accomplishments of His people.

In most homes where there are school–age children, an art gallery of sorts doubles as a refrigerator in the kitchen. On it hangs some of the most creative works of art the world has ever seen. Green dogs, brown sky, tracings of tiny hands, crayon squiggles—all priceless treasures, not because they can fetch millions at auction by snobbish collectors, or because they represent "a refreshing adaptation of post–modernism resurgence in a third–grade renaissance." They are valuable because they were made by our kids, and we love them, and we celebrate each victory and achievement in their young lives.

One night after I put my little girl to bed and had some quiet time to think, I had a strange image of a huge refrigerator door where God displays all our little victories with great affection and pride. He displays for all to see the times we reach out to Him and love Him and share our faith with others.

I do not see an angry, demanding God who is never pleased; I picture God showing our lives and victories through His Son, to all the assembled multitude around the throne amid all of the singing, light and glory. "Come see what they did for Me, for My children, for My Son today. Come, let's celebrate!" The Lord knows how!

Lessons from Lincoln

We would think that a man of Lincoln's prominence in history must surely have had something memorable in his pockets on the night he died. This is what they found:

- a handkerchief embroidered "A. Lincoln"
- one small penknife
- a spectacle case repaired with string
- a small purse containing a Confederate $5 bill
- several old, well–worn newspaper clippings.

The clippings, obviously read and reread many times, were articles from the English press that praised Lincoln for his speeches, his character and his efforts to govern the United States through a time of crisis. He treasured these reviews since most of the press, north and south alike, more often attacked rather than praised him.

If ever a man in a place of responsibility felt alone and in need of encouragement, it was Abraham Lincoln. Not only did he carry the burden of a nation at war with itself but he led a life and political career marked more by failure and frustration than victory:

1831—failed in business
1832—defeated for a seat in the Illinois state legislature
1833—failed at business ... again
1834—elected to legislature
1836—proposed to Mary Owens and was turned down
1838—defeated for speaker
1840—defeated for elector
1843—defeated for Congress
1846—defeated for Congress
1855—defeated for Senate
1856—defeated for Vice Presidency
1858—defeated for Senate
1860—elected President of the United States

1864—re–elected to the Presidency
1865—first American president to be assassinated.

Lincoln's private life was not without its troubles, either. Mary Todd Lincoln, a headstrong, spoiled woman of substance, never missed a chance to remind her husband that she could have done better in her choice of a mate. She tried to make old Abe into someone more genteel and refined, contrary to his natural homespun plainness. Sons Edward and William died as children. Tad, who survived the White House years, died at age 18, leaving only Robert to outlive his parents.

Why would Lincoln subject himself to such pain when there were other options open to him? I think it was because he viewed his work for the country, to hold the fragile union of our republic together, worth any price or sacrifice. He saw the daily casualty reports and felt the full weight of the war effort as if he alone carried the burden for the Union's survival.

The Apostle Paul showed similar strength of character in the face of difficulty and opposition. He saw Christians being martyred and others falling away from faith and felt a similar burden for the building of Christ's kingdom. From prison he wrote in 2 Timothy 1:15 that "everyone in the province of Asia has deserted me." Some of his friends were away on active service, leaving only Luke to help. He was alone with the burden of the new church and its leaders and had no one but God to share the load.

Paul says in his letter to Timothy, "At my first defense, no one came to my support ... but the Lord stood at my side and gave me strength, so that through me the message might be fully proclaimed" (2 Tim. 4:16–17). Alone and apparently unsupported, without even a few tattered newspaper clippings for solace, Paul was confident that "the Lord will rescue me from every evil attack and will bring me safely to His heavenly kingdom" (v. 18).

The rewards for Paul's miraculous conversion and worldwide missionary travels seem dubious at best. Five times he received 39 lashes. He was stoned by the Jews and left for dead. Three times he was beaten with rods, and three times he was shipwrecked and spent a night and a day on the open sea, no doubt suffering from seasickness (2 Cor. 11:24–30). He constantly lived on the move and in danger—from storms, bandits, his own countrymen, false brothers and the Gentiles. Paul says he "labored and toiled" (2 Cor. 11:27) for the sake of the gospel, often going without sleep, food, shelter or warm clothing. And on top of everything else, he felt the almost crushing pressure of his concern for the newly founded churches and their brand–new Christian believers. Eventually he was executed for the cause of Jesus Christ.

Paul, like Lincoln, considered his God–given task worthy of sacrifice. Let us take encouragement and challenge from this great president's second inaugural address:

"With malice toward none, with charity for all, with firmness in the right as God gives us to see the right, let us strive on to finish the work we are in, to bind up the nation's wounds, to care for him who shall have borne the battle and for his widow and his orphan, to do all which may achieve and cherish a just and lasting peace among ourselves and with all nations."

To that the Apostle Paul would say, "Amen."

Fishers, Not Hunters

"As Jesus was walking beside the Sea of Galilee, He saw two brothers, Simon called Peter and his brother Andrew. They were casting a net into the lake, for they were fishermen. 'Come follow Me,' Jesus said, 'and I will make you fishers of men.' At once they left their nets and followed Him" (Matt. 4:18–20). Jesus called Peter and Andrew to be fishers of men. As His disciples we are called to the same mission.

In the area of Pennsylvania where we once lived, two special days on the sportsmen's calendar come close to rivaling even Christmas and Easter: the opening days of the deer and trout seasons. Thousands of avid outdoorsmen take to the field with joyful enthusiasm, never worrying about time, cost, family or jobs, as the thrill of the sport and the enjoyment of the outdoors keeps them interested and invigorated.

But why are we called to be fishermen in our Christian witness and service and not hunters?

In order for hunters to be successful, they have to bring home something dead. It is very difficult to sneak up on a trophy buck and say, "Tag, you're it," while a friend takes a photograph for posterity. Whether you hunt big game, small game, birds or varmints, success as a hunter means something has to die.

A hunter uses weapons that allow him to shoot his game from fairly long distances while concealed in the undergrowth and camouflage. The point is to make sure that the prey does not see the predator until it is too late.

It is difficult for the animal to learn any useful or positive lesson from the hunting experience. Old bucks get to be old bucks because they learn to stay away from man once they hear the guns on opening day. But before the animal learns the lesson, it may already be too late.

Hunters and fishermen both use bait. Hunters in recent years have taken to using scents that duplicate the smell of a doe in heat, capitalizing on the aggressive sex drive of the male deer.

However, fishermen, with the exception of those who go out on the deep sea, tend to stay fairly close to their quarry, realizing that if they can see the fish, the fish can see them as well. They use lures and baits that resemble food or something that piques the fish's curiosity. A piece of corn, pork rind, minnow or fat worm may not appeal to your culinary tastes, but to a big trout it is gourmet dining at its finest.

The fish, once hooked, can be smarter for the experience. The fish has felt the sting of the hook, the pressure of the line that leads him where he did not want to go and the prospect that his future would involve heat and bread crumbs. He may be only slightly hurt from the ordeal, but he is definitely smarter. Next time he will not be so eager to chase after the first tasty morsel that catches his eye.

Jesus said that He came to give life and to give it in abundance (John 10:10). That is why we are called to be fishers and not hunters. We present the gospel of Christ that comes as appealing, satisfying nourishment for the soul to those who are empty and hungry. We use that message of love and redemption not as a weapon to kill their spirit but as a lure to attract them to a loving Savior who wants to meet their needs and who gave His own life to redeem them from the penalty of sin. Jesus never used the hunter mentality to count victories in terms of trophies dead and mounted on the wall, but to give life and life to the full to those who desperately long for it.

The biggest fish are down in the depths. That is where you have to drop your line if you ever hope to catch the really big ones. Jesus went to the depths to search out the worst sinners who needed His forgiveness the most.

Like a fish on a hook, we have known the pain of sin, with its entrapment. We know what it is to be held captive against our will to patterns of addictive behavior. We have also known the healing pain of conviction that confronts us with the truth about ourselves. It makes us hurt enough to stop sinning and to allow Jesus to forgive us and to take control.

Do you remember when you first accepted Christ into your life? Like most you probably fought it all the way—wriggling, squirming, making excuses, running, leaping and thrashing in an effort to exercise your own rebellious nature, until finally you submitted to His loving forgiveness. Most amazing of all, once you submitted and accepted His will and His love, He set you free—to love and to win others.

"Blood and Fire" or "Semper Fi"?

In her article "Has the Fire Gone Out?" Commissioner Flora Larsson asked if the fire of the Holy Spirit has somehow gone out of the ministry of The Salvation Army. She did not suggest that we had completely lost our values but that we may have replaced the spiritual energy and evangelistic ardor of our early years with a comfortable and respectable orthodoxy—one that was acceptable to our people and to those who support the work of the Army with their donations.

Perhaps to avoid of the risk of losing the fire, we might consider trading mottos with the United States Marine Corps. The oldest arm of the military of the United States has long been recognized and remembered by their motto of *Semper Fidelis*, which means "always faithful." And they have been, at Tripoli, the Ardennes, Iwo Jima, Tarawa, Beirut. They have been the first to fight and often the first to die in defense of the United States. They have been faithful to their commitment to the marine corps and to their country.

But given the occupation of warfare, might not "Blood and Fire" suit them better than it does us? They are in a business that sheds blood and uses fire both to preserve life and to take it. Maybe "Blood and Fire" suits them since it speaks of might and power as well as sacrifice and destruction.

The Marines take great pride in their strength and preparedness, as well as in their reputation for service in the most difficult and dangerous circumstances. They take great pride in having a "can do" attitude—the willingness to take whatever risks or make whatever sacrifice necessary to achieve victory. They often serve as shock troops, assaulting an enemy–held territory, meeting the stiffest resistance and fiercest battle. Theirs is a literal "baptism of fire" in the face of enemy guns to secure a beachhead for the reinforcements to follow.

They know that theirs is a fairly elite corps since so much is demanded of them. They know that they are "the few—the proud," and they thrive on being where the fighting is the heaviest.

The Salvation Army's motto "Blood and Fire," as any Junior Soldier can tell you, stands simply for the blood of Jesus Christ and the fire of the Holy Spirit. The blood refers to the atonement of Jesus Christ; He chose to die for the sins of mankind so that we might be restored to a loving relationship with God. The fire is the purifying fire of God the Holy Spirit which prepares us to be the people of God. Early–day Sunday evening salvation meetings were called a baptism of fire—not the fire of rockets or bombs but of the Holy Spirit. Salvationists eagerly sought the infilling power of God for fellowship with Him and for soul–winning ministry. Have we, over the years, lost the energy and drive we once had? Have we lost the baptism of fire?

Commissioner Larsson suggested that "Blood and Service" might be a more fitting motto since we are known internationally as a major human services provider. Or perhaps "Blood and Program," since we have skill and character–building activities for every age group, from the cradle to the grave. I only hope we are not "Blood and Smoke"—with only the appearance of fire, but no passionate heat.

Three things are necessary for fire—oxygen, heat and something to burn. In the Christian sense we need three things for spiritual combustion— the Holy Spirit of God, a heart warmed by His love, and a life willing to be set on fire by that love. Anything less may be only smoke with no fire.

Maybe *Semper Fi*—always faithful—suits us better? We are faithful to our schedule of activities; faithful to our traditions; faithful to the uniform; faithful to the community's high regard for our reputation of kindly service; faithful to providing assistance to those in desperate need without discrimination; faithful to providing relief for those in crisis; and faithful to the design and intent of The Salvation Army as an evangelical movement.

The Marines are faithful to the service of their country regardless of personal risk or hardship. And we in The Salvation Army are faithful to the Lord Jesus Christ who redeemed us from sin by the shedding of His blood and by the empowering of His Holy Spirit, who calls us to be the people of God to serve and to win others to His kingdom.

We are rightly concerned with church growth in The Salvation Army. But we will never see any real growth, regardless of scientific methods and strategies, if the Holy Spirit does not provide the fire. Without Him we are spiritual pyromaniacs bent on making fire without the Lord. We are trying to jump–start the church with our own batteries and our own power without the all–consuming, all–powerful fire of God.

I think we should stick with the motto that has served God and mankind all these years. We may also need to return to some of our ways of daring and the "can do" attitude exhibited by some early Army pioneers.

Take heart. The Lord, like the Marines, is still "looking for a few good men"—and a few good women, a few good boys and a few good girls to rally to the "Blood and Fire."

Wait for
the Gift

"Lord give me patience ... and give it to me now!" That plea accurately describes our society which seems to be stuck on fast forward.

We hate to wait for anything. A delay of a few seconds at a traffic light seems like an eternity. Scientists have discovered that the shortest space of measurable time is the time it takes the New York City cab driver behind you to lay on the horn after the light turns green. For some people (usually men), waiting for a few commercials on TV is an unbearable ordeal that can only be remedied by zapping the remote to see every program in quick succession. Men call it channel surfing—women call it infuriating.

If we get impatient with a book we are reading, we skim it and skip to the last chapter to see how it turns out. But that is exactly what Jesus told the disciples not to do. In order to give this nearly powerless handful of believers all the encouragement possible, they needed to wait for the gift of the Holy Spirit. Jesus warned them not to go on until they had received the gift of His power. If they jumped ahead, they might learn how the story ends, but they would not be part of the adventurous ministry spreading in ever–widening circles around the world.

Following the resurrection, Jesus' disciples asked, "Lord, are You at this time going to restore the kingdom to Israel?" They thought that this would be the ideal opportunity to establish the kingdom of God on earth and drive out their Roman oppressors once and for all. Instead Jesus told them, "It is not for you to know the times or dates the Father has set by His own authority" (Acts 1:6,7). He also told the disciples to "wait for the gift My Father promised, which you have heard Me speak about" (Acts 1:4). That gift was the Holy Spirit—the living person, personality and presence of Jesus Christ.

Impatient disciples like Peter may have thought that staying in Jerusalem to pray was a colossal waste of time, wishing rather to get on with the work ahead.

A professor who was trying to teach patience and the importance of following directions instructed, "Do not answer any questions until you have read through them all." The last question said, "If you have nothing on this exam paper but your name, please turn it in. You are finished." It was painful to watch students frantically erasing answers to questions they were told not to answer.

Fortunately for us and for the message of the gospel the disciples did wait and did receive the gift as promised. They met in deep prayer and were filled with the Holy Spirit who came with gale–force winds and sheets of flame to hover over each person. The confirmation of that infilling came shortly thereafter when the disciples preached in languages they had never studied and were understood by all. It would be much like speaking and being understood at the United Nations without benefit of translation.

But the real miracle was in the complete transformation of Peter as he preached his first sermon. This was the same man who had three times denied that he even knew Jesus. Now he spoke eloquently, logically and persuasively. I can imagine people asking, "What got into him?"

What got into Peter was the Holy Spirit. Some in the crowd looked for a simple solution by saying that he was drunk. Peter stood and quieted their derisive laughter. "Fellow Jews ... Let me explain this to you" (Acts 2:14), as he quoted from the prophet Joel. He gave an impassioned and strangely scholarly message, hinging the gospel on the resurrection of Jesus Christ as the key point of all Christian theology. He was not at all afraid to declare that "God has raised this Jesus to life, and we are all witness of the fact ... be assured of this: God has made this Jesus, whom you crucified, both Lord and Christ" (Acts 2:32, 36).

Scripture states that when they heard this, they were wounded to the heart. The Holy Spirit convicted them of their lost and sinful condition. Almost as an afterthought, Luke writes that many repented and were baptized and that about 3,000 new converts joined the church after that first sermon.

"Every good and perfect gift is from above, coming down from the Father of the heavenly lights" (James 1:17). No strings, no fine print, and no "offer void where prohibited." We claim it when we wait and are yielded to the Lord and ready to receive the gift of the Holy Spirit.

What is required is an open heart, a stubborn self–will yielded to Jesus Christ and a faith to believe that God can and will deliver the gift of the Spirit as He promised. What a wonderful gift! And one well worth waiting for!

Weapons and Warriors

Much of the Old Testament deals with wars, campaigns and conquests by the nation Israel and her enemies. We know very well that the Lord used vast armies to rout the enemies of Israel and to teach Israel to be obedient to God by learning from defeat.

They had none of the hi–tech weapons we have today. A few years ago the word "patriot" was the generic name for one who professed a devotion to one's country, or the name of a troubled football franchise. We know the word now as the name for anti–missile missiles. Thanks to news coverage from around the world, we have seen other weapons in action—smart bombs, cluster bombs, cruise missiles and all manner of projectiles guided by television, laser, radar and wire. Some can be launched from hundreds of miles away and be guided right through the front door of the target building. Modern combatants can fight each other from miles away with rocket and artillery, never seeing the enemy firsthand. But in Bible days, war was waged man to man. You could see, smell, hear and touch the one who was as intent on taking your life as you were on saving it.

Weapons were made of copper, wood, bronze, and in the case of the Philistines, iron. Iron was superior because it was harder and held a cutting edge better than the other metals. The possession of iron weapons made Philistia a major military power, often at Israel's expense. Swords, clubs, spears and arrows were the chief armaments of the day. In fact, for all of our technological preoccupation with new and improved instruments of destruction, all we have improved is the delivery system that allows men to kill more efficiently than ever before—spears to arrows, arrows to bullets, bullets to missiles.

But reading through the Bible we see that God often chose non–traditional weapons used by specially chosen people to defend His people. He often used small and insignificant weapons and warriors to do great things for Him.

Gideon was no career military man. All he wanted was to be left in peace, but if that wasn't possible, he wanted to do the Lord's bidding to rid Israel of the Midianites. He qualified as a patriot in the best sense of the word. Judges chapter 6 tells us that with a force of only 300 men armed with trumpets and clay pots containing lit torches, Gideon attacked the superior army of Midian, creating such chaos that the Midianites killed each other in the melee. God used a small force commanded by a brave man given completely to the Lord's work, so that all would know God was the Victor.

Joshua marched around the heavily fortified city of Jericho six times in total silence in front of the massed array of the Canaanite defenders. On the seventh and final pass, the priests blew trumpets with such a blast from God that the walls fell flat without air strikes, cruise missiles or smart bombs.

In Judges 3 Ehud, the judge who dispatched evil King Eglon of Moab, is notable not for his choice of weapon, but for the fact that he was left-handed. Being a southpaw would have been reason to be rejected from military service in a right-handed world. His superiors saw everything as backwards, but the Lord looks with different eyes.

Shamgar the judge and the son of Anath saved Israel by killing 600 Philistine invaders using an oxgoad for a weapon (Judg. 3:31).

There are other famous warriors with strange weapons. Mighty Samson killed 1,000 men while armed with nothing more than the jawbone of a donkey (Judg. 15). And nearly every Sunday school child knows how David defeated Goliath with only a sling and five smooth stones. Confident that he and the Lord were such good marksmen, David left the remaining four stones for Goliath's four brothers!

But how many know about little Jael, the house-, or rather, tent-wife? Following a major rout against the armies of Israel, Sisera, commander of the army of Jabin of Canaan, ran for his life. In his flight he found refuge in Jael's tent. He asked her for water but instead she gave him warm milk that made him feel relaxed and sleepy. And while the great general lay sleeping, Jael took a mallet and a tent peg and fastened Sisera to the floor. I love the KJV rendition of the event that says she "smote the nail into his temples, and fastened it into the ground ... so he died" (Judg. 4:21). Talk about understatement!

It is notable that the Lord used a housewife with a simple weapon to deliver Israel from the hands of their oppressors. He chose Israel to be His special people not because they were so powerful, but because they were so small among other nations. Jesus took 12 mismatched men and built the foundation of the Christian Church that has spread the gospel of Christ all around the world. He took the offering of one little boy with five barley loaves and two small fish and fed a multitude over more than 5,000 people.

That is the way that God works. He takes a little and does great things with it. "But God chose the foolish things of the world to shame the wise; God chose the weak things of the world to shame the strong. He chose the lowly things of this world and the despised things—and the things that are not—to nullify the things that are, so that no one may boast before Him" (1 Cor. 1:27–29).

Paul had the right idea when he understood that any power for ministry or life in general came from the Lord and not from our own store of creativity and charisma: "But [Christ] said to me, 'My grace is sufficient for you, for My power is made perfect in weakness'" (2 Cor. 12:9).

The Lord does great things with unusual weapons and insignificant warriors, provided they are given completely to the Lord's service. Maybe He has something special for you and me, too.

One Plus God =
A Mighty Army

I must admit that living out Christianity on a day–to–day basis can be a bit lonely at times. Scripture tells us that the Holy Spirit comes to assist us, since His very name means "One called alongside to help," but it would be encouraging if the Lord put flesh and blood on His assistance.

Hebrews 12:1 says, "since we are surrounded by such a great cloud of witnesses, let us throw off everything that hinders and the sin that so easily entangles, and let us run with perseverance the race marked out for us." I haven't identified many "clouds of witness" lately, although I could sure use the help.

In some Scripture passages, Paul gives encouragement by reminding us that we are part of the body of Christ, with each component interdependent on the other. "The body [of Christ] is a unit, though it is made up of many parts; and though all its parts are many, they form one body" (1 Cor. 12:12).

At times we can pray, serve and evangelize in the company of other believers who give us strength and encouragement. But more often, we are called on to live out our faith on a purely individual basis. Once in a while, I'd like the Lord to give me a vision of the physical presence, human or angelic, of the "cloud of witnesses" [teammates] available to help when I feel overwhelmed. Every now and then, the Lord does just that by allowing His people to catch a glimpse of the magnitude of His team.

One of those occasions is recorded in an odd little story in 2 Kings chapter 6. Ben Hadad, King of Aram, planned to raid the northern kingdom of Israel and steal the best the country had to offer. As a king and military leader, he was shrewd and ruthless. But he didn't have Elisha—the man of God in Israel.

Every time Ben Hadad planned a raid, Elisha warned the king of Israel to make defensive preparations as if every word spoken in King Hadad's strategy sessions was transmitted to the prophet Elisha and then to the king of Israel. What fabulous military intelligence!

After being thwarted several times, Ben Hadad turned his attention away from raids to the more pressing matter of terminating this bothersome prophet. He sent armies, archers, chariots and soldiers of every kind to get Elisha. "Bring me the man of God and I don't care how you do it. But bring him to me—now!"

Within a few hours, a huge army surrounded the small town of Dothan, where the prophet lived, and set up their siege. Dothan, an essentially undefended rural community, was encircled by a huge security force bent on arresting one humble prophet.

Early in the morning, Elisha's servant came to warn his master of the assembled troops around them. You or I would panic or run!

"Don't be afraid," Elisha replied. "Those who are with us are more than those who are with them" (2 Kings 6:16). I wonder what the servant thought when he looked all around seeing only his master while feeling like the Lone Ranger and Tonto against the whole world.

"'O Lord, open his eyes so he may see' ... Then the Lord opened the servant's eyes, and he looked and saw the hills full of horses and chariots of fire all around Elisha" (vs.17).

The two of them and the "cloud of witnesses" had the army surrounded! It is good that in answer to Elisha's prayer the Lord permitted the army to be temporarily blinded and led away from Dothan without loss of life. Elisha may have had a difficult time advising them to "Drop your weapons and come out with your hands up. We have you surrounded."

But even better than having an angelic army or a cloud of witnesses to protect us in battle, we have Jesus Himself. He promised that "I am with you always, to the very end of the age" (Matt. 28:20), through all of the things we face in our lives right now. We may feel at times that it is us against the world with no one to help us. But with Jesus, we are an unbeatable team.

Forever Your Friend

Television and feature films have given us a window on the friendship between Star Trek's James T. Kirk and Lt. Commander Spock who have explored "strange new worlds" and "boldly gone where no one has gone before." These two have fought Klingons, Romulans, Tribbles, androids and the like from one end of the universe to the other.

In *Star Trek II: The Wrath of Khan*, we lost Spock. He was killed by a massive dose of radiation while resetting the warp engines so that the crew might avoid being blown to galactic dust. (Unlike our earthbound reality, Hollywood brought Spock back to life for *Star Trek 3–6*.)

As he was dying Spock told Kirk that "There are times when the needs of the many outweigh the needs of the one." Logic dictated that one should die to save the rest. He also reminded Kirk in a painful farewell that "I am now, and forever shall be, your friend." And with his typical splay–fingered Vulcan salute he gave up his life with a weak "live long and prosper."

Scripture records a similar friendship between David, the anointed and soon–to–be–crowned King of Israel, and his best friend, Jonathan, son of King Saul. Theirs was a friendship that could only be severed by death itself.

Dear David,

Tomorrow our army goes out to fight the Philistines at Mt. Gilboa. It is a poor location for a battle since it is so difficult to defend. We are significantly outnumbered. But worst of all, my father the king does not have the leadership necessary to win the day. I fear that this is a campaign from which very few of us will return.

I have known battle before, and I have no fear except that I cannot help but imagine that things will not go well for us. I hope you will remain in a place of safety, since your life as God's anointed is too valuable to be spent on such a futile lost cause as this.

You have seen the changes in my father over the years. Once he was confident and assured—he was every bit the king. But now he has slipped into madness. I still remember the days when he would listen to your singing and get great pleasure from it. Those days at the palace when we were young and shared our adventures and our dreams were the best years of my life.

More than ever I am confident that you are indeed God's man for the task of king of Israel. Some have said that I should be angry that you have taken what should be mine as Saul's first born. But I know you are the right choice. I think Saul is going into this battle looking forward to a release from himself.

Take care of my family when I am gone. My only regret in all of this is that I will miss you, my friend. But there are times when the needs of the many outweigh the needs of the few ... or the one. Better that you remain the leader that neither Saul nor I could ever hope to be.

I am now, and ever shall be, your friend.

Live long and prosper.

                                        Jonathan

One Samuel 31:1-2 records that Saul, Jonathan, his brothers Abinadab and Malki-Shua and many of the army of Israel were killed the next day in action with the Philistines at Mt. Gilboa. And David never forgot the friend who was closer than a brother.

Scripture also records that Jesus loves us with a love greater and stronger than that of a brother or a friend. It is even stronger than death.

"As the Father has loved Me, so have I loved you. Now remain in My love. My command is this: Love each other as I have loved you. Greater love has no one than this, that he lay down his life for his friends. You are My friends if you do what I command ... I have called you friends, for everything that I learned from My Father I have made known to you" (John 15:9,12-14).

I am now, and eternally shall be, your friend. Live long and prosper.

                                        Jesus

Decisions, Decisions, Decisions

All day, every day we make decisions. Big ones, small ones, ones that sometimes are important and many that are not. That is why when I go out to dinner for a relaxing evening with my wife, I don't want to spend the whole time making decisions.

As soon as we walk into the restaurant, the questions and the choices begin.

"How many?" the hostess asks to the two of us standing there.

"Two," I reply, wondering who else she sees.

"Smoking or non–smoking?"

"Non–smoking please," I say, glad that they don't have a place for chewers and dippers.

At last we reach our table and begin to check out the menu. In this particular place there are about 475 different items to be decided upon. After a reasonable length of time our waiter comes to the table to take our order.

"Good evening. My name is Pierre and I will be your server tonight."

Great, I think, *I need a server for tennis practice, not for dinner. His name was Pete when he worked at the chili place.*

Pierre goes on, "Let me tell you about our specials for the evening," as he lists enough choices to complicate an already gargantuan menu. But we have already decided what we want, and to Pierre's dismay, our choice is not one of the 78 specials he has memorized and quoted.

You would think that was the end of the decision–making process. No such luck, for now we have to decide on salad dressing—Italian (creamy, or low–calorie), thousand island, French, blue cheese, Russian, ranch, honey mustard, vinaigrette, pepper garlic, poppy seed, sweet and sour or vinegar and oil.

"What kind of potato? Mashed, baked, french fries, homefries, boiled ..."

"How do you want your steak prepared? Well, medium, rare ..." I'd like to say "edibly," but I don't think he'd get it.

"Please choose four of the following 38 vegetables ..."

Finally the order is done—or so you think. Invariably one or more of the items is out of stock and you have to change it. And of course Pierre, or

Pete, comes back 10 or 12 times to ask, "Is everything all right?"

Just leave me alone so I can eat, all right?

But after all of this, the most important decisions may not have been answered. The most important choices you will ever have to make are "What will you do about the Lord?" and "What will you do about your sin problem?"

Scripture is filled with people who chose poorly when given a serious decision to make: our first parents, Adam and Eve, who chose to disobey God; Cain, who decided to murder his brother Abel; Saul, who decided not to follow the direct instruction of the Lord in the matter of the defeat of the Amalekites; Judas, who chose to betray Jesus.

The Bible reveals good choices as well, by those who accepted Jesus' offer of redemption: lepers, prostitutes, cripples, tax collectors and other common sinners of all social classes. In light of Jesus' love, they chose wisely to accept grace and peace rather than nagging guilt, light rather than darkness, hope rather than despair, life eternal rather than perpetual damnation.

Acts 16 records the decision of the jailer in Phillippi who was guarding Paul and Silas. When a massive earthquake rocked the jail, opening the cells for a potential escape, he asked quite simply, "Sirs, what must I do to be saved?" And the single option was presented: "Believe in the Lord Jesus and you will be saved—you and your household" (Acts 16:30–31).

Paul and Silas did not present the entire menu of Christian doctrine and tradition but gave the opportunity to accept Jesus Christ by grace through faith. It must have been enough information, for a few verses later "the jailer brought them [Paul and Silas] into his house and set a meal before them; he was filled with joy because he had come to believe in God—he and his whole family" (Acts 16:34).

Of all the decisions we make, the choice to accept Jesus as Savior is the most important one we will ever make. A very wise decision indeed.

CREST BOOKS

Salvation Army National Publications

Crest Books, a division of the Salvation Army's National Publications department, was established in 1997 to produce books with a solid biblical foundation and a compelling message on holiness, in keeping with the Army's roots in the Wesleyan tradition. Listed here are the 12 titles published to date, as well as our theological journal *Word & Deed: A Journal of Salvation Army Theology and Ministry.*

Never the Same Again
by Shaw Clifton
ISBN: 0-9657601-0-3

Christians are sometimes overwhelmed by what they feel are confusing explanations of the deeper aspects of faith. The author makes these readily understandable by drawing on his thorough knowledge of Scripture to help seekers establish a sure foundation. Clifton encourages new believers' enthusiasm for Christ while guiding them through roadblocks that can stunt spiritual growth. He addresses such questions as: Can I be sure I'm saved? How much like Jesus can I be? Will God equip me to serve Him? Can I rely on God? This is an ideal resource for new converts, individuals making recommitments, seekers looking to know more about the Christian faith and leaders of discipling groups.

Romance & Dynamite: Essays on Science and the Nature of Faith
by Lyell M. Rader
ISBN: 0-9657601-5-4

"Whatever God makes works, and works to perfection. So does His plan for turning life from a rat race to a rapture." This and many other anecdotes and insights on the interplay of science and faith are found in this collection of essays by one of The Salvation Army's most indefatigable evangelists. As a Salvation Army officer, the author used his training as a chemist to prove the absolute trustworthiness of the Bible, find evidence of the Creator's hand in everything natural and scientific and demonstrate why the saving knowledge of God is crucial to understanding life's value and purpose.

Celebrate the Feasts of the Lord
by William W. Francis
ISBN: 0-9657601-2-X

Author William Francis presents an examination of the feasts and fasts established by God in Leviticus 23, as well as those inaugurated after the Babylonian exile. With studied skill, he examines the historical background of each feast and makes clear its significance for the modern Christian. This book meets a critical need by revealing how Jesus participated in the feasts during His earthly life and how, in Himself, their meaning was fulfilled. Study guides follow each chapter, allowing readers to explore and apply the new insights, and making this book ideal for group study.

A Little Greatness
by Joe Noland
ISBN: 0-9657601-4-6

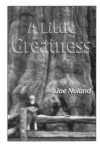

Under the expert tutelage of author Joe Noland, we explore the book of Acts, revealing the paradoxes of the life of a believer. We can know "common wonders," practice "defiant obedience," be "lowered to new heights" and assert "gentle boldness." Using word play and alliteration, Noland draws the reader into the story of the early Church and reveals the contemporary relevance of all that took place. The book is divided into three parts, which address shared aspects of heavenly greatness available through the help of the Holy Spirit: great power, great grace and great joy. A Bible study and discussion guide for each chapter helps the reader apply each lesson, making this an ideal group study resource.

Pictures from the Word
by Marlene Chase
ISBN: 0-9657601-3-8

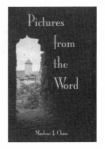

"The Bible is full of beautiful word pictures, concrete images that bring to life spiritual ideas," writes Chase. For instance, "God's personality is poignantly revealed to us in such images as a hen sheltering her chicks or a loving father engraving the names of his children into his hands. These and a host of other images teach us about God and about ourselves." In 56 meditations, the author brings to life the vivid metaphors of Scripture, illuminating familiar passages and addressing the frequent references to the vulnerability of man met by God's limitless and gracious provision.

Christmas Through the Years:
A War Cry Treasury

ISBN: 0-9657601-1-1

Through the years, the pages of the Christmas *War Cry* have proclaimed the timeless message of the birth of the Babe of Bethlehem. *Christmas Through the Years* contains articles, stories, poetry and art that have inspired readers over the past half century. This treasury highlights Salvationists of wide appeal from General Evangeline Booth (1948) to today's eloquent international leader, General John Gowans, and also features contributors such as Billy Graham and Joni Eareckson Tada.

Easter Through the Years:
A War Cry Treasury

ISBN: 0-9657601-7-0

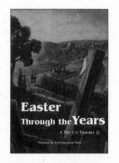

A companion volume to *Christmas Through the Years*, this treasury of work culled from the Easter *War Cry* over the last 50 years will recount the passion of Christ and uniquely unpack the events surrounding the cross and the numerous ways Easter intersects with life and faith today. Contributors include Joni Eareckson Tada, Max Lucado, Commissioner Samuel Logan Brengle and General William Booth.

Who Are These Salvationists?
by Shaw Clifton
ISBN: 0-9657601-6-2

Clifton has written a seminal study that explores
the Army's roots, theology and position in the body
of believers and provides readers with a definitive
profile of Salvationism and Salvationists. This study
will help Salvationists to understand their historical
and theological roots and shape their understanding of the Army's
mission in the new century. The book will also provide non–
Salvationists with the most comprehensive portrait of the Army and
its soldiers produced to date and will introduce them to the theology
which drives our social action.

He Who Laughed First: Delighting in a Holy God
by Phil Needham
ISBN: 0-8341-1872-6

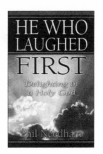

This invigorating book is the first joint–venture
publishing project undertaken by Crest Books and
Beacon Hill Press. Needham questions why there are
so many sour–faced saints when the Christian life is meant to be
joyful. In his book he explores the secret to enduring joy, a joy that
is not found by following some list of prescriptions, but by letting
God make us holy, by letting Him free us to become who we are in
Christ: saints. *He Who Laughed First* helps the reader discover the why
and how of becoming a joyful, hilarious saint.

Slightly Off Center! Growth Principles to Thaw Frozen Paradigms
by Terry Camsey
ISBN: 0-9657601-8-9

As an established expert in the field of church health, Camsey seeks to thaw frozen paradigms of what is "Army." He challenges us to see things from a different perspective, thus throwing our perspectives slightly off center. Camsey urges us to welcome a new generation of Salvationists whose methods may be different than those of the Army of the past, but whose hearts are wholly God's and whose mission remains consistent with the fundamental principles William Booth established. *Slightly Off Center!* is ideal for stimulating discussion in group settings and will encourage corps officers, soldiers and corps councils to renew their vision and fine–tune their purpose and ministry.

Our God Comes: And Will Not Be Silent
by Marlene Chase
ISBN: 0-9704870-0-2

Our God Comes rests on the premise that, like the unstoppable ocean tide, God comes to us in a variety of ways and His voice will not be silent as He reveals Himself throughout all Creation. This book of poetry, the first of its kind for Crest Books, invites the reader to contemplate life's experiences and God's goodness to us. An accomplished writer and poet, Chase offers a book that lends itself to devotional meditation, small group discussion and the literary enjoyment of carefully crafted poetry.

A Salvationist Treasury
by Henry Gariepy
ISBN: 0-9657601-9-7

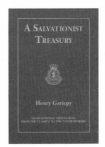

This book brings to readers the quintessence of devotional writings from Salvationist writers spanning over 100 years. From Army notables to the virtually unknown, from the classics to the contemporary, this treasure trove of 365 inspirational readings will enrich your life, deepen your devotional study and enhance your grasp of the Army's principles and mission. *A Salvationist Treasury* is certain to become a milestone compilation of Army literature.

For order information, contact the Supplies and Purchasing department nearest you:

Atlanta, GA—(800) 786–7372
Des Plaines, IL—(847) 294–2012
Rancho Palos Verdes, CA—(800) 937–8896
West Nyack, NY—(888) 488–4882

Word & Deed: A Journal of Salvation Army Theology and Ministry

Now in its third year of publication, *Word & Deed* has become a respected voice in the ongoing discussion of Army theology and ministry. Volume one featured the doctrine of holiness, a fundamental tenet of Salvationism, while volume two addressed ecclesiology and the Army's place within the Christian Church. Volume three addresses holiness and community, synthesizing the topics of the first two volumes. This theme is continued in the Spring 2001 issue of *Word & Deed* (vol. 3, no. 2).

Volumes four and five will include papers delivered at the International Theology and Ethics Symposium at William and Catherine Booth College in Canada.

Take part in the discussion—subscribe today!

Yes, please begin my subscription to *Word & Deed: A Journal of Salvation Army Theology and Ministry*.

❒ Gift*
❒ 1 year (two issues) – $18.00
❒ 2 years (four issues) – $36.00

Name _____

Address _____

City _____

State/Province _____ Zip _____

Country _____

*Donor (if gift) _____

*Please list additional gift subscriptions separately. International orders: Canadian subscribers add $4.00 per year for each subscription. All other international subscribers add $8.00 per year per subscription. Back issues are available; please contact the circulation manager to obtain your copies of volumes 1–3.

Enclose check or money order payable to The Salvation Army (U.S. currency only, U.S. funds drawn on U.S. bank). All subscriptions must be pre-paid. Billing is not available. Send to: Circulation Manager, National Publications, P.O. Box 269, 615 Slaters Lane, Alexandria, VA 22314. For payment by credit card, contact the Circulation Manager at (703) 684-5500, or via email at cwilson@usn.salvationarmy.org.